Collisions, Deflections, and Conjunctions

Aşkın Çelikkol

Collisions, Deflections, and Conjunctions
The Representations of Turks and Moors in Italian Folktales

PETER LANG

**Bibliographic Information published by the
Deutsche Nationalbibliothek**
The Deutsche Nationalbibliothek lists this publication in the Deutsche
Nationalbibliografie; detailed bibliographic data is available online at
http://dnb.d-nb.de.

Library of Congress Cataloging-in-Publication Data
A CIP catalog record for this book has been applied for at the
Library of Congress.

This project is supported by
TÜBİTAK- International Postdoctoral Research Fellowship Program.

ISBN 978-3-631-85476-1 (Print)
E-ISBN 978-3-631-85477-8 (E-PDF)
E-ISBN 978-3-631-85721-2 (EPUB)
E-ISBN 978-3-631-85722-9 (MOBI)
DOI 10.3726/b18528

© Peter Lang GmbH
Internationaler Verlag der Wissenschaften
Berlin 2021
All rights reserved.

Peter Lang – Berlin · Bern · Bruxelles · New York · Oxford · Warszawa · Wien

This publication has been peer reviewed.

www.peterlang.com

Acknowledgments

This book would not have been possible without the support of a few individuals who have helped me to pull through many obstacles and difficult times. I would like to express my gratitude to Prof. Sergio Bozzola for hosting me at the University of Padua and for his kind support during my stay in Italy. I am also grateful to Prof. Hasine Şen Karadeniz, Prof. Hürriyet Özden Sözalan, Assoc. Prof. İnci Bilgin Tekin, and Asst. Prof. Sinem Yazıcıoğlu who took time to review my drafts and took care of the bureaucratic nuisances that would otherwise hamper the progress of my work.

Table of Contents

Introduction

If there is an Other, whatever or whoever he may be,
whatever may be his relations with me, and without his
acting upon me in any way except by the pure upsurge of
his being – then I have an outside, I have an essence.

––Jean-Paul Sartre, *Being and Nothingness*

In 1598 crescent bearing banners glimmered on the horizon of the Mediterranean Sea steadily approaching the island of Sicily. For the islanders, the sight, albeit nerve-wrecking, was a usual one as they suffered the relentless incursions of the corsairs from the Barbary Coast operating under the dominion of the Ottomans or the occasional attacks of the Sultan's fleet that patrolled the territorial waters of Italy. In that particular moment, however, the vessels sailing into the port of Messina did not carry ill-intent but the good-will of *Kapudan Paşa*, the admiral of the Ottoman navy, Ciğalazade Yusuf Sinan who wished to meet with certain inhabitants of the island (Graf 1). The petition to be granted permission to hold a private conversation with a select circle of islanders may sound strange at first glance given the enmities that existed between the Ottomans and the Italian city states. However, a second look at Ciğalazade Yusuf Sinan Pasha's life history should explain away a portion of the strangeness of the incident. Born in 1544, Scipione Cicala was a son of a Genoese nobleman, whose wealth depended on the lucrative operations of piracy, and at the age of fourteen Scipione was captured, along with his father, by the Barbary corsairs and sent to Istanbul. Entering into the *devşirme* system of the Ottomans, an educational institution that trained young Christian boys for the Janissary corps or the bureaucratic administration, Cicala converted to Islam and was given the Turkified name Yusuf Sinan and his patronym Cicala was likewise adapted to his new identity and Ciğalazade, meaning Cicala's son in Turkish, was granted in recognition of his status. Ciğalazade Yusuf Sinan quickly rose through the ranks of the Janissary Corps and became a Yeniçeri Ağası (a rank roughly equivalent to modern day's captain or to a centurion in the Roman army). His administrative skills while in the elite military unit did not go unnoticed and Yusuf Sinan was rewarded with the office of grand vizier and was later appointed as the admiral of the Ottoman Navy. The cloud of mystery why Yusuf Sinan Pasha wanted to meet with a few islanders might have cleared by now, but the question as to the composition of the company rowed to the admiral's ship and the rumors as to the content of the conversation need to be further addressed.

For Henry Lello, the English ambassador to Istanbul from 1597 to 1607, Ciğalazade arranged a meeting with his family members, his brother and mother, either to discuss his possible return to Christianity and to his fatherland or the relocation of his family in Istanbul. On the prospect of Ciğalazade's repatriation to Italy, some sources claim that the Pope Clement VIII pinned his faith on the admiral's shift of allegiance and had the younger brother Carlo to deliver a message that asked Yusuf Sinan to abandon the Ottomans and join his Christian brethren in their crusading campaign against the infidel Turks. Obviously, the Pope's call fell on deaf ears since Yusuf Sinan continued to serve the Ottoman Sultan until his death in 1605. In Lello's account, another conjecture on the content of the meeting is given and it is quite an intriguing one. It is claimed that Yusuf Sinan met with his mother on that day to take her with him to Istanbul. Some sources state that Ciğalazade's mother was an Ottoman Muslim and was abducted by his corsair father while navigating the Mediterranean. Probably, Yusuf Sinan wanted his mother to see her motherland once again and to drop the charges for apostasy by reasserting her Muslim identity. Whether Ciğalazade succeeded in bringing her to Istanbul or that was his intention all along are subject to speculation and except for ambassador Lello's account no historical data exist to validate the story.

In Christian Europe, the renegades were not looked upon favorably as they were regarded to be apostates relinquishing the faith of their forefathers for an impostor religion. The converts were accused of treachery and treason and were even held in a stronger contempt than Ottoman Turks. Matteo Zane, the Venetian ambassador in Istanbul in 1594, branded the defectors as "the most arrogant and evil men imaginable, having lost, along with their true faith, all humanity" (Graf 29). In all likelihood, Zane's views were influenced by the affluent life style the converts enjoyed and Zane, perhaps tinged with envy, perceived it to be a sign of corruption. Seconding Zane's thoughts and reiterating the trope of sordid renegade, Václav Vratislav of Mitrovic (an official in Hapsburgs' embassy) wrote of Ciğalazade in the following manner: "having once tasted Turkish freedom and pleasures, [he] proceeded gradually to worse and worse, till now he will have nothing to do with Christianity; but, on the contrary ... is a great enemy of the Christians" (Graf 32). To become *Turk* or to turn *Turk* (farsi *Turco* in Italian) was no simple matter limited to the idiosyncrasies of some stray Christians but a problem that had to be addressed at the state level. Queen Elizabeth's good relations with the Ottomans and the Moors of Morocco elicited harsh criticism from the Pope and her opponents in Britain. She was accused of being in "a confederate with the Turks" for making trade deals with the Ottoman Empire and of tarnishing the "immaculate" identity of Anglo-Saxons for opening the borders to Turks and Moors. In fact, a nascent and yet growing Muslim community was residing in Elizabethan London and was comprised of interesting figures such as "Turkish ex-prisoners, some Moorish craftsmen, a number of wealthy Turkish merchants. . .a 'Moorish solicitor,' as well as 'Albion Blackamore, and the Turkish Rope-daunser'" (Dalrymple xix).

The irrefutable presences and legacies of the Christian converts in the Ottoman Empire such as Ciğalazade Yusuf Sinan (Scipione Cicala), Uluç Ali (Giovanni Dionigi Galeni), Gazanfer Agha (the Venetian chief eunuch), Hasan Agha (Samson Rowlie), Fatma Hatun (Beatrice Michiel), Ali Bey (Melchior Tierberg), Mahmud Bey (Sebold von Pibrach), Hurrem Sultan (Anastasia/Aleksandra Lisowska, wife to Suleiman the Magnificent and mother to Sultan Selim II) point beyond the bipolar and the confrontational model Bernard Lewis and Samuel Huntington have tailored for so-called Judeo-Christian and Muslim blocs. For Lewis and Huntington, Christianity and Islam, and for that matter the Western and the Eastern worlds, were locked in a mortal struggle for supremacy from the seventh century onwards and this tug-of-war even continued into the twenty-first century as epitomized by September 11, 2001 attacks. The fixed, monolithic vision of history Lewis and Huntington espoused was later challenged, and is still vehemently criticized, by historians who put forward counter researches that argued for hybrid identities, intersecting cultures, and porous frontiers to study the encounters between the Christian (Western) and Islamic (Eastern) worlds. Among such works the notable examples can be listed as follows: *Re-Orienting the Renaissance: Cultural Exchanges with the East, Turks, Moors, and Englishmen in the Age of Discovery, Venetians in Constantinople: Nation, Identity, and Coexistence in the Early Modern Mediterranean, Creating East and West: Renaissance Humanists and the Ottoman Turks, Renegade Women: Gender, Identity, and Boundaries in the Early Modern Mediterranean, The Sultan's Renegades: Christian-European Converts to Islam and the Making of the Ottoman Elite, 1575–1610, The Black of Florence: The Spectacular Life and Treacherous World of Alessandro de' Medici.*

For all its intentions to move Ottomans and Moors into focus and to dismantle "clash of civilizations" thesis, existing scholarship on the Ottomans and the Moors has remained broadly historicist in method. The scholarship has laid the groundwork for the reintegration of the Ottoman and the Moorish presences into the historiography through detailed accounts of Mediterranean power struggles, the incursions of the Ottomans into Central Europe, diplomatic exchanges between Venice and Istanbul, and the operations of the North African corsairs sailing under the Ottomans' banners. As Pascal Firges and Tobias Graf point out, the counter "bloc paradigm" scholars have "only scratched the surface. . .[of] understanding the driving forces behind the long-standing

intensive exchanges between individuals and groups of different ethnic, religious, and social origins" (7). One can argue that only a small part of transnational exchanges has been dealt with, for, to reiterate, scholarship has largely
been limited to historiography and assigned secondary and supportive roles to
literary texts. On the part of the studies that feature Turkish and/or Moorish
characters, the literary works that find place are mainly comprised of plays and
pageants and a systematic study of these primary sources can be found in Early
Modern English Studies. Focusing on the representations of Turks and Moors in
English literature and on the English stage, Mark Hutchings' *Turks, Repertories,
and the Early Modern English Stage*, Warner G. Rice's *Turk, Moor, and Persian
in English Literature from 1550–1660, with Particular Reference to the Drama*,
Steven Mullaney's *The Place of the Stage: License, Play, and Power in Renaissance
England*, Anders Ingram's *English Literature on the Ottoman Turks in the Sixteenth
and the Seventeenth Centuries* and *Writing the Ottomans: Turkish History in
Early Modern England*, Gerald MacLean's *Culture and Society in the Stuart
Restoration: Literature, Drama, History*, Daniel Vitkus's *Turning Turk: English
Theater and the Multicultural Mediterranean, 1570–1630*, Matthew Dimmock's
New Turkes: Dramatizing Islam and the Ottomans in Early Modern England com-
prise the bulwark of the literature. The relatively large quantity of works that thus
characterize the Early Modern English History and Literature cannot be found
in other European nations.

On the Ottomans and their representations in Italian literature only
a handful of books and articles can be found and there is no available study
conducted to explore the Moors in Italian literature. Oğuz Karakartal's *Türk
Kültüründe İtalyanlar* (2002) (*Turks in Italian Culture*) and *Türk Edebiyatında
İtalyanlar* (2003) (*Turks in Italian Literature*), Ümit Gürol's *İtalyan Edebiyatında
Türkler: Başlangıcından 1982'ye* (1987) (*Turks in Italian Literature: From the
Beginning to 1982*), Erol Makzume's *Osmanlı Topraklarında İtalyan Oryantalistler*
(2007) (*Gli orientaliasti italiani nel Territorio Ottomano*), Marina Formica's
*Lo specchio turco: immagini dell'altro e riflessi del sé nella cultura italiana d'eta
moderna* (2012) (*The Turkish Mirror: Images of the Other and Reflections of the
Self in Modern Italian Culture*) can be counted among the few sources that constitute the corpus. As can be inferred from their titles, the foci of some of these
works are not entirely on literature, and literary works are used as complementary sources for studies on culture and history. Ümit Gürol's *İtalyan Edebiyatında
Türkler: Başlangıcından 1982'ye* could be singled out as an exception since the
study offers a compendium of literary depictions of Turks in plays, novellas, and
lengthy poems (poema). Unfortunately, Gürol's work relies on monolithic and

dualistic readings that divide the Ottomans and Italians into clashing Oriental and Occidental blocs.

The invocation of the current monograph is not to reclaim the Turks and the Moors for Eurocentric perspectives nor for Orient based political histories but to show how Turkish, Moorish (Muslim), and Italian (Christian) characters are implicated in reciprocal questions of fantasy and projection. For that matter, the monograph moves the Ottomans, the Moors, and the subaltern populations of Italy into focus and grant them the central stage via Italian folk tales. The book does not deny the import of history in addressing literary works, specifically folk narratives, and makes use of the discipline as propounded by the literary theory "new historicism." Based on the assumption that a study of a socio-cultural milieu is crucial for a profound understanding of a work of literature, and a close study of a literary work is equally significant in acquiring a deep comprehension of a cultural period, the book combines history and literature and seeks to analyze cultural discourses and literary texts as parts of a network of hegemonic struggles for domination and resistance.

The first chapter "A Survey of Theory" offers a survey of the main theoretical strands in folklore studies and discusses the strengths and weaknesses of each perceptual framework. The chapter broaches the subject of history and discusses the respective positions of the "communicative model," the Finnish historical-geographical method, Formalism, Structuralism, and Psychoanalysis on the use and import of history in folkloristics. The chapter provides the reasons why these methodologies do not hold history as pertinent register in the studies of folklore or why they regard history to be inexpedient discipline to address folktales. The following sub-section "Straddling History and Literature" seeks to counter the arguments raised by the theories and posits history as an integral part of folk literature and proposes an interpretative model that combines historical accounts and folk narratives. The final sub-section "The Other's Mirror" commences with a brief overview of the functions of mirror in folk literature and concludes with a discussion that in Italian folktales the figures of Other, Turks and Moors, operate as reflective surfaces that cast back the clashing, bifurcating, and intersecting paths of the ruling classes and the subaltern groups.

The second chapter opens with a half-historical and half-fictional story of a janissary who seeks refuge and eventually settles in a town in northern Italy. The janissary whose legacy is still visible today is a popular figure on account of his heroic stand against the oppressive regimes of local landlords. The story or the legend of Hasan the janissary is an epitome of the peculiar position of Turks in the imaginary landscape of Italy as his inclusion still retains his foreign status and corresponds to certain uses in sociopolitical and sociocultural modalities.

Concerning the Ottomans, it is near impossible to speak of a concerted political stance in Italy during the fifteenth and the sixteenth centuries for the city states had their unique political aspirations and the Ottomans were either cast as the most potent enemies of Italian Catholicism and were portrayed as savage, treacherous worshippers of a fiendish religion or as valuable trade partners and strong allies against the rival regional powers. The first part of the chapter undertakes to address such equivocal historical accounts on the Ottomans and progresses with the analyzes of the folktales endeavoring to answer the questions whether the folk narratives adopt the circulating negative or positive traits attributed to the Ottomans or whether the tales map an alternative reality that points beyond the canopy of official historiographies.

The last chapter begins with a brief historical account of Moors in Italy and cites certain cases whereby Moors and Ottomans are used somewhat interchangeably. The chapter provides explanations for the political motivations of such attempts at conjoining Moorish and Turkish identities and mentions a few counter arguments that assign different roles to Moors and Turks in Italian cultural history. Compared to the "arch nemesis" or "useful enemy" tropes ascribed to Turks, Moors are postulated as proximate and yet dangerous presences within. Regarding the alternative and/or counter sites of reality of folk tales, an argument similar to the one made in the preceding chapter is repeated in this chapter with certain twists. Moorish characters featured in the folk tales are studied under the leitmotifs of death and slavery. These recurring themes pervade the studied folk narratives and the Moorish characters face social and physical death in the progressions and the conclusions of the tales. In this regard, despite certain themes traversing the representations of Turkish and Moorish characters, slavery and death are highlighted as the major markers of difference, and thus an analytical frame that diverges from and yet sustains the theoretical backdrop provided in the second chapter is offered.

In the opening epigraph, Jean-Paul Sartre identifies the Other as a pedestal figure who, by means of her/his sheer presence, brings forth one's *raison d'être* and as a linchpin that holds together a complex and yet a fragile *beingness*. Sartre's insight may not suffice to explicate *raisons d'état* of nations and empires, let alone the interethnic, intra-racial relations and hybrid identities spreading over vast territories and spanning long stretches of time. In the history of Europe, however, the existence of Other has been instrumental in forging and consolidating a continental identity. The Renaissance scholars, drawing on Hesiod, Xenophon, Herodotus and other ancient Greek writers, pictured Europe as a realm of change and reform against a static and conservative backdrop of the East (Neumann and Welsh 335). Muslims, Moors, and Turks were fitted in the latter category and correlated with the watershed moments in the European history that paved the way for the emergence of an overarching European identity that was coterminous with the notion of the Occident. Besides strangers that were spatially outside the sovereign borders, there were also "internal Others" who protruded through the social fabric. Availing themselves of both the passive and active elements in culture, passively incorporating the ideologies and values of an authority and actively re-working those values and offering their counter-ideologies, and occupying the contradictory positions of "acceptance" and "resistance," "isolation" and "collectivity," "disunity" and "cohesion," the subaltern peasant groups dovetailed with the definition of "domestic stranger" (Arnold 30).

The story of Cicala family, of Yusuf Sinan and of his nameless mother in particular, punctures a hole in the endeavors to resuscitate the ages old practices of discrimination and to press identities into clashing geographical zones and further reveals the latent fears of "turning" of "going to the other side." Moreover, the family nicely encapsulates the seemingly contradictory positions of outside and inside, strange and familiar, consent and dissent, and ultimately stands for non-orientable, convoluted relations that are difficult to fasten to a binary. *Collisions, Deflections, and Conjunctions: The Representations of Turks and Moors in Italian Folktales* is about such anecdotal histories and folk tales that provide windows on the numerous interconnections between Turks, Moors, Italian peasants and lords; between nations, communities, and individuals whose pathways crisscrossed the fictitious and the factual landscapes of Otherness marked by stories and histories of enmity, captivity, exile, death, love, and reunion. The study does not refute the tangible effects and evidences of politics of dualism on Western and Eastern cultures, the politics that have persisted through different epochs in similar forms, but approaches the issue of Other from an angle that conjoins the presences of "external Others," Moors and Turks, with the tales of "internal Others," Italian subalterns, to throw a light on the convoluted hegemonic relations between different strata in the Italian society in the fifteenth and the sixteenth centuries. The book argues that in Italian folktales, Turks and Moors function both as symbolic lapses mirroring the fears, anguishes, and the defects of the Italian society, and as anchoring points co-opted by the ruling classes to preserve the delicate equilibrium of hegemonic alliances. Combining history and literature, the study contends that Italian folktales present sites of contestation in which miscellaneous class positions and discourses vie with one another for ascendancy, and Turkish and Moorish characters enter into such struggles for power as conduits for subjugation and/or as mediators between discordant and incompatible social realities.

I. A Survey of Folklore Theories

In a Jewish story quoted *in extenso* by Giorgio Agamben, Baal Schem – the founder of Hasidism – would pay a visit to a particular location in the woods, get a fire going, meditate and pray for the righteous path to take for the difficult task at his hands. After a generation of the late Schem, Maggid of Meseritz, would go to the same spot, pray in meditation but would see no need for a fire. Yet in another generation following Meseritz, Rabbi Moshe Leib of Sassov, weighed down with the same task, would follow the trajectory of his forerunners and find the sylvan space but would dispense with the fire, the meditation, and the prayers, thinking it sufficient nonetheless. When Rabbi Israel of Rishin, the last Talmudist, is summoned to perform the task, he ensconces himself in his golden chair and simply responds that it is now impossible to light the fire, to say the prayers and to know the place, "but" he adds, "we can tell the story." For Agamben, the gradual loss of the fire, the prayers and the place brings about the "liberation of the tale from its mythical sources" and paves the way for "the establishment of literature." Such liberation and distancing from the sources of mystery, however, also give way to an amnesia about the memory of the fire; the fabular element of tradition. On the other hand, the element in which mystery is "dispersed and lost" is history, in other words, rather in the words of Giorgio Agamben, "history [storia] is that in which the mystery has put out or hidden its fires." Agamben posits that the only way to approach the lost enigmatic kernel is by traversing the mist of history, which leaves the researcher with a paradox to mount: "where there is the tale, the fire is out; where there is the mystery, there cannot be the story" (Agamben 1–2).

The conundrum of underplaying the historical import of the tales while attempting to keep track of the glimpses of the recondite fire, or in Jack Zipes's words "casting a magic spell" over this "vital quality of the tales," has proved to be the bone of contention for numerous researches conducted in folkloristics (Zipes 26). The methodological turn to "ethnography of communication," to participatory and performative dimension of folklore, has tackled the dilemma by arguing for multiplicity of social identities and their interactions over particularism of a hegemonic social position and its monoculturalism. Alan Dundes's "units of worldview" hypothesis that foregrounds the study of small groups as the proper line of inquiry, William Hugh Jansen's "esoteric-exoteric factor"; formations of in-group self-images vis-à-vis the reflexive apperceptions of an outer group, Richard Bauman's "communicative interaction" model conceptualizing the protean and differential characteristics of a folk group, Dan Ben-Amos's treatment of folklore not as a projection (as a "mirror" of a literary genre or of a cultural era) but as a process, enabling "a sphere of interaction in its own right," have addressed the heterogeneous, fluid, and porous identities that characterize the multicultural societies in the contemporary world.

Dan Ben-Amos in particular addressed the seemingly exclusive categories of folklore and history and further posited that they constituted the fulcrum around which the discussions on the definition of folklore turned. If a folklorist would dedicate her/himself to the salvage of tradition from the wreck of oblivion, s/he then had to face the dilemma of becoming an "antiquarian from which he tried so hard to escape." Ben-Amos maintains that to avoid such fate, the definition of folklore itself should be re-calibrated and expanded to admit "broader and more dynamic research in the field" (Ben-Amos 12–14). Nevertheless, the definitions, as Ben-Amos further notes, have been tinged with a certain interest and yet with a sense of denial as disciplines have paid attention to the "exotic" subject of folklore without acknowledging it to be a part of their expertise. Anthropologists held folklore to be the subject matter of literature, while the scholars of literature defined it as a cultural topic and therefore inscribed it in the profession of anthropology. If any study of folklore would be undertaken by those disciplines, it would play a minor and supportive role and would at best be treated as a "mirror" of a literary genre or of a cultural era.

Auspicious as Ben-Amos's suggestions are, some uncertainties yet exist as to the implications and implementations of the communicative process in cultural, literary and political contexts. One of the primary, or perhaps the main, questions would be on the nature of such interaction: if a reciprocal influence or a set of influences should be the governing dynamics in folklore studies, to what extent conflicts of interests (literary, cultural and political) should be accounted for in a critical study of folklore? Another crucial and relevant question can be posed for the agency of folklore in sociopolitical matters especially when cultural politics become the site in which myriad identities, discourses and viewpoints come into play for a hegemonic position. Should folklore then, as Americo Paredes claimed, be situated at the heart of the cultural studies as a response to a volatile political milieu?[1] If the answer is affirmative, should we also follow in

---

1 For further reference and discussion on the politics of folklore and cultural studies, please see Charles L. Briggs's journal article "What We Should Have Learned from Américo Paredes: The Politics of Communicability and the Making of Folkloristics," published by *The Journal of American Folklore*.

the footsteps of Richard Bauman who upheld the "communicative interaction" model as the most effective way in conceptualizing the protean and differential characteristics of a folk group; in comprehending its lore as "an instrument of conflict" as well as "a mechanism contributing to social solidarity"? (Bauman 38).

For Bauman, a Turkish street vendor's cry selling fabrics for ladies "Run, ladies, run! Run to fabrics without tearing one another to pieces! Printed calicoes! Let's give the reds, the purples! Flowers of the seven mountains! Come, ladies and gentlemen! What your eyes see and what your hearts like are all here" (Uysal 204) is a fine example of folkloric performance in which identity differences centered on occupational diversities between the seller and buyer come to the fore. Still, the vocational markers are somehow eliminated since the vendor's cry includes a conflict of interests, and also a performance for "solidarity," simultaneously playing "different, complementary. . . .as well as parallel roles" (Bauman 34). William Hugh Jansen's "esoteric-exoteric factor" addresses a similar case of "isolation" and "communication," where "the esoteric applies to what one group thinks of itself and what it supposes others think of it," whereas "the exoteric is what one group thinks of another and what it thinks that other group thinks it thinks" (Jansen 205–206). Jansen's formulation, also based on a communicative model, nevertheless presumes a stricter and a less permeable boundary between an inner and an outer group. An esoteric group, an African-American group for instance, may very well know the exoteric, white American views regarding its community, and the African-Americans are free to either accept, or reject, or tolerate those outer group perceptions. Jansen makes an interesting observation at this point that some of "American Negro tales collected from Negroes may be based upon obviously white, i. e. exoteric, concepts of Negro characteristics," and in a similar vein, "the most pernicious anti-semitism appears in Yiddish jokes told by Yiddish comics" (Jansen 206–207). It can be inferred then, from Jansen's words at least, that the inner-group incorporates even the most segregationist jokes about itself but has almost no qualms about accepting and conveying them.

Such imputation on the part of the esoteric groups that have been historically and culturally trodden on and at times subjected to systematic violence sounds problematic in certain respects. Primarily, it ignores the painful in-group memory that is shaped by ineffable experiences of the Middle Passage, slavery, the Holocaust, and the pogroms. Secondly, by effacing the traces of such experiences, Jansen puts the in-group – outer-group communication in a somewhat non-conflictive zone, void of any exploitative, power-ridden traces of interactions.

Practical and convenient in certain regards, the methodological turn to "ethnography of communication" and to social processes is nevertheless inclined to discard the influence of tradition on the lore of a group and tends to offer synchronic studies of micro-communities that are formed around a particular event or an organization, a football match or a club (Dundes, 1980), or around an act, "self-formation through consumption" (Noyes 22) in which participants examine their identities through appropriation and expropriation of cultural commodities. American scholars, in their attempt to throw off the yoke of Eurocentric methods, have shifted the focus from hierarchic to communal identities, yet, in doing so, they have posited history and tradition as unfeasible and inessential categories (Noyes 21–23).

In Europe, scholars did not fare better than their U.S. counterparts in resolving the dilemma of history and mystery, Finnish historical-geographical method, best exemplified by Stith Thompson's Tale Type Index, premises that a tale found in numerous other versions has a particular place and time of origin and is produced by a deliberate act. This originative act journeys in "wave-like" formations and while it expands in ever widening circles, the act catches on and is caught by secondary implications and interpretations. The Finnish method, as Richard M. Dorson propounds, rejects the sweeping theories of diffusion that rely on "polygenesis or independent inventions. . .dream origins, ritual origins, origins based in observation of heavenly phenomena, or in the savage mentality, or as the expression of repressed infantile fantasies" (Dorson 94). The method also takes issue with anti-diffusionist approaches that set up linguistic and cultural impediments to historical and geographical diffusions of the tales and claims that a tale can easily climb over the linguistic and cultural fences and further posits that the itinerary of a tale consists of a journey from advanced to less developed civilizations.

Despite being a dominant strand in folklore studies today (Dorson 93), the Finnish school was criticized by a number of formidable scholars of the field. The assumed Ur-type indexing of the tales; the speculative supposition that the variants of a tale hark back to a source, was highlighted for criticism. The Swedish scholar Carl Von Sydow believed that provincial histories and local cultural factors shaped the form of an international tale, not the other way around, and those local formations retained their unique, distinctive historicities, Von Sydow called them *oikotypes*, despite partaking of an international tale[2] (Von Sydow 11–43). Other significant scholars, Reidar Christiansen and Laurits

---

2   Von Sydow challenged the hypothesis that the original form of a folktale was necessarily the most complete, most logical version although he confessed this had been his own view when he began his folktale research.

Bødker criticized the Finnish method for its uncompromising and somehow automated disposition for reducing "tale studies to statistical abstracts, summaries, symbols, tables, and maps, ignoring aesthetic and stylistic elements and the human side, of the narrator" (Dorson *Folklore and Folklife* 9).

On the movement of folk tales from a so called civilized world down to underdeveloped regions, Stith Thompson has the following remarks to make: "If the principle is really valid we may ask whether tales must keep running downhill culturally until they are found only in the lower ranges" (Thompson 438). Alan Dundes regards Stith Thompson's view in particular and the Finnish method's approach in general as devolutionary on the grounds that both Thompson's approach and the school's methodology regarded the original version to be complete whereas the shorter versions, as the original offshoots to renditions, "are assumed to be fragments." For Dundes, the transition from a supposed "perfection" of the original to the "imperfect" adaptations subsequently introduced a "deep resentment of change and an equally deep-seated resistance to the study of change in folklore" (Dundes 8). Stith Thompson believed that such resistance to change was especially crucial as when "a change of detail is made in a story it is undoubtedly a mistake, an error" (Thompson 437), contaminating a text by deleterious additions and memory lapses and thus making it ever difficult to reach, to work backwards, to an unadulterated *Urformen*.

The concerns that revolved around the finding of an original *Ur*-form glossed over, as can be easily surmised, some of the vital issues that needed to be addressed at some length. Giving the Finnish method its due, for its protracted and exhaustively meticulous annotations, Richard M. Dorson nevertheless points out that the critical issues such as "the mysterious processes of creation and alteration, of the influences of national cultures, the social context" were lost in the maze of tables and indexes. For Bruce A. Rosenberg, Vladimir Propp came forth to sort out the imbroglio of the Finnish school; to "redress the mid-1920s' Finnish murkiness" (Rosenberg 92). Despite the Finnish School's adherence and claim to strict indexing of the tales, Propp regarded the School's classifications to be somewhat undifferentiated bundles in which iniquitous characters are held to be coterminous with and at times replaced by fiends or animals, thus indiscriminately attributing identical qualities to humans, animals, and objects. In the way of a rectification and a criticism, Vladimir Propp introduced an alternative sequential arrangement that gave credence to form over content. Assigning the former with a constant and an immutable task in the analyzes whereas positing the latter as arbitrary and mutable entities, Propp designated thirty-one functions or narrative units; functions that served as "stable, constant elements in a tale, independent of how and by whom they are fulfilled" (*Morphology of the*

Folktale 10). Thus, Propp's morphological study of folktales rendered it possible to make international, transnational interpretations of the tales in question in which a "Swedish King is easily replaced by the Turkish Sultan" (Propp *Theory and History of Folktale* 28).

Perhaps the harshest criticism leveled against Propp's views came from Levi Strauss. Strauss's critique was centered on two main points: Propp's formalist methodology lacked a historical dimension,[3] and his methodology treated tales as the residues of already defunct, archaic myths. Strauss, on the other hand, maintained that the relationship between a folktale and a myth was not "that of anterior to posterior," nor of "primitive to derived," but of a complementary nature. He further noted that if folktales were to be studied in isolation from the myths they originated, they were fated to move like "a satellite without a planet," eventually losing the grip on the orbit they followed.

> The point is not to choose between the tale and myth but to realize that they are the two poles of a field that also includes all sorts of intermediate forms and that their morphological analysis must be the same, or else one may miss elements belonging to the same system of transformations. (*Structural Anthropology* 178)

By stressing the significance of nonantagonistic and compatible study of folktales and myths, Strauss also set a marker between formalism and structuralism:

> For formalism, the two areas must be absolutely separate, as form alone is intelligible, and content is only a residual deprived of any significant value. For structuralism, this opposition does not exist; structuralism does not treat one as abstract and the other as concrete. Form and content are of the same nature, amenable to the same type of analysis. Content receives its reality from its structure, and what is called form is a way of organizing the local structures that make up this content. (*Structural Anthropology* 179)

To get his point across, Levi-Strauss cited Native American narratives, which offered different functions of different trees, not limited to and restricted by the archetypal concept of tree. For Levi-Strauss, the significance, or the "concrete realizations" of the plum tree and the apple tree could not be categorized under "arbitrary" perceptions of the natives and therefore reduced to "one function of which the tree is only a support" (*Structural Anthropology* 182). Not a formalist but a contextual analysis would eventually reveal that plum tree was important for the indigenous community for its productivity and the apple tree for its

---

3 In response to Strauss, Vladimir Propp admitted that his methodology lacked historical research and literary criticism, and yet he adhered to formalist position and posited it as a prerequisite for any historical and critical effort to be made. Please see *Theory and History of Folklore*, 1997, p. 78.

durability. In this sense, structuralist approach to folktales, to folklore in general, proposed an analytical framework that was not based on a monolithic, homogeneous understanding but on a heterogeneous, polylithic one in which distinct functions or features depended on a manifest or a latent underlying structure.

At this point, a question similar to Gilles Deleuze's inquiry in *Desert Islands and Other Texts* on how to recognize structuralism should be posed so as to further unbutton and address some of the key issues related to the structuralist methodology. Gilles Deleuze enumerates seven criteria to recognize and identify the structuralist thought despite the diversity of the works penned by numerous scholars. These criteria should be allotted some space since structuralism holds a key position in understanding and attending to the main theoretical debates found in folklore studies today.

The first criterion in "How Do We Recognize Structuralism?" is perhaps one of the most important tenet of Structuralist thought. Behind, and spatially speaking, under the mantle of imaginary and the façade of social reality, "a third order, a third regime: that of the symbolic" can be found at work. The "positing of a symbolic order, irreducible to the orders of the real and the imaginary, and deeper than they are" is the biggest discovery of structuralism and it is "defined. . .by the nature of certain atomic elements which claim to account both for the formation of wholes and for the variation of their parts" (Deleuze 173). From Marxist to Psychoanalytical and Formalist literary theories, this symbolic structure can be found in various forms and is utilized for different purposes. Louis Althusser's reading of ideology and of ideological interpellation, for example, can be said to be based on such implied, unconscious inscription of oneself into the symbolic, read ideological, network. For a transition from an individual to a subject of ideology, it is imperative to respond, to allude oneself, however unconsciously to the hail "hey you!" ringing behind one's back (Althusser 264). Jacques Lacan's famous triad of Imaginary, Symbolic and the Real is also based on a symbolic structure in which "symbolic as element of the structure constitutes the principle of a genesis" and the symbolic structure, deeper than the real and the imaginary, functions as "the substratum both for the strata of the real and for the heights *[dels]* of imagination" (Deleuze 171).

The fourth criterion that should be addressed at some length is the coexistence of differential and at times of contradictory elements within a structural organization. For Deleuze, structures are always unconscious and virtual (non-actual) to the extent that they are "real without being actual, ideal without being abstract" (Deleuze 101). Thus, Deleuze reasons, Claude Levi-Strauss often presents a structure "as a sort of ideal reservoir or repertoire, in which everything coexists virtually, but where the actualization is necessarily carried out according to exclusive rules, always implicating partial combinations and unconscious choices" (Deleuze 179). In this regard and if writ large, the society can also be posited as "the total structure of a domain as an ensemble of virtual existence" and the "substructures" found within the domain "correspond to diverse actualizations" (ibid.). Hence, it can be understood why Levi-Strauss assigned different (differential) functions/actualizations to "plum" and "apple" trees within the totality of Native American mythology. The implications of the fourth criterion could be further extended and be explained by a recourse to Alan Dundes's allomotifs and to Psychoanalytic study of folk tales.

Alan Dundes's "allomotifs" can be compared with Vladimir Propp's "narratemes" in terms of their similar approach to the substitutability of characters in a folk narrative. As mentioned before in the Swedish King and the Turkish Sultan analogy, Propp holds a character in a folk narrative to be an insignificant, lesser unit of a narration so long as it fulfills a certain function within the overall organization of the narrative. In this respect, if a narrative foregrounds a theme of heroic features and feats; wisdom, goodness, sacrifices, struggles etc., regardless of the character's characteristics and for that matter of its individual properties, an archetype precedes subjectivity and thus a tzar, a khan, a king or a sultan may interchangeably be used for the given type or the "narrateme." Similarly, Alan Dundes appropriates this notion of interchangeability, however, unlike Propp, Dundes stresses the psychological components of a narrative, and thus extends the range of substitutive variations to include not only the characters but also the magical objects and the narrative units. For instance, if a hero comes into possession of a magic ring that may grant him extraordinary powers, the ring may stand in for the symbolic equivalent of a phallus, or if the hero is robbed of this ring, then it may be possible to surmise that an act of castration is inflicted on the hero and thus his emasculation is sealed.[4] Alan Dundes, somehow egressing from the mainstream Psychoanalytical analysis, explains and validates his approach in the following sentences:

> Again, please note that these alleged equivalents come from versions of the tale type, not from some armchair Freudian analyst. We may or may not choose to believe a psychoanalyst who tells us that decapitation can be a symbolic substitute for castration, but we simply cannot ignore the relevant evidence from folklore itself. The folk, collectively, are

---

4   Emasculation by castration is one of the commonplace themes found in various mythological texts from ancient Mesopotamia, Egypt, and Greece. The replacement of a "tyrannical" Deity (Father) by other deities (son(s) or a wife) is an overarching subject matter often narrating a regime change in the pantheon. On the subject, please see David Adams Leeming's *The World of Myth* anthology.

giving us a range of allomotifs which structurally speaking must be considered as functional equivalents. (*Parsing through Customs* 174)

Ernest Jones, a long-time friend of Sigmund Freud, delivered a speech before the
Jubilee Congress of the Folk-Lore Society in 1928 on the uses of Psychoanalytic
theory and its application in folklore studies. Jones claims that certain parallelisms
can be drawn between folklore and the unconscious mind: "We find the people
concerned with such matters as the preservation of health, the warding off of
danger and death, the hopes of fortune, and the desire for happy marriage and
the blessing of children. The unconscious is similarly engrossed with such topics
and in even more primitive terms" (15). To exemplify his claim, Jones cites the
example of the Devil as the atavistic father figure who is traditionally associated
with the snake and thus is depicted in a folktale with a double function: "The
devil, whose phallic symbolism is evident in his frequent identification with a
snake, is a father figure incarnating two repressed wishes, the desires of the son
to both imitate and defy his father" (250). Carl Gustav Jung, another close friend
and a student of Freud, can be cited as the most well-known scholar whose
archetypes are often used as reference points in folklore studies. Jung's archetypal
motifs and images (the apocalypse, the great flood, genesis of the world, father-
mother couple, the wise old man/woman, trickster, healer etc.) and his notion
of the collective unconscious that ascribes a universal mental state reaching as
far back as to the stone age, have proved to be useful categories to explicate the
folktales from a psychoanalytic perspective.

The scholars utilizing psychoanalysis to analyze folklore have made use of
Freudian symbolism and of Jungian archetypes to interpret their material and
have even come the conclusion that fairy tales and folktales were therapeutic for
infants and adults alike to deal with traumatizing experiences. Verena Kast in her
book titled *Folktales as Therapy* and true to her Jungian standpoint argues that
folktales, tailored to the modern conditions in due course, offer symbolic support for those who suffer from devastating psychic traumas or struggle with daily
concerns, anxieties, and stress. Bruno Bettelheim's *The Uses of Enchantment: The
Meaning and Significance of Fairy Tales* makes a similar assumption about the
good use folktales can put to in resolving psychic and mental disorders, and even
helping develop in children a sense of ". . .achieving a more mature consciousness to civilize the chaotic pressures of their unconsciousness" (23).

The shift of focus from the individual to the social processes, or rather the
integration of the private domain with that of the public; the conjoining of
psychoanalysis with sociology have opened up new venues for the analysis of
folktales. Such paradigm shift sought to disperse some of the criticism levied

against psychoanalytic literary theory and aimed at creating a dynamic, interdisciplinary theoretical frame. J.L. Fischer, in his lengthy article *The Sociopsychological Analysis of Folktales* draws attention to the collaboration of social and psychological processes in creating complementary works on folklore. For Fischer, the distinction "between types of tale as to reflection and distortion of reality, however, is a matter of degree" and a folklorist should not heed this "matter of degree" not of a kind difference but instead pay attention to a joint study of folklore from sociological and psychoanalytical perspectives (239). Ruth M. Boyer nicely encapsulated this new theoretical position by offering a new understanding and approach to myths and folk stories.

> The myth is a special form of shared fantasy that serves to bring the individual into relation with members of his cultural group on the basis of common psychological needs. It can be studied from the point of view of its roles in fostering both psychic and social integration. As a form of community illusion, not only does it assist in alleviating individual guilt and anxiety, but it adds to the cohesion of the social group and constitutes a form of adaptation to reality. It thus influences the development of both the sense of reality and the superego. (428)

Undeniably, the theoretical strands and methodologies that have been given consideration in the preceding pages have contributed a great deal to the corpus of works and to the wide array of subjects written in the fields of folkloristics, cultural studies and comparative literature. The communicative model that purports to study an inner group's and an outer group's conscious and unconscious perceptions of themselves and of one another, thus prioritizing the study of micro-communities over larger entities such as nations, has facilitated an interest in groups that have been overlooked and pushed to the periphery of society or in communities that have vegetated in the privileged central zones of race and ethnicity. The scholars of this method have certainly helped to reconfigure and change the reception of folk culture and popular culture that have been traditionally relegated to less significant subjects of study or have been treated as appendages for seemingly more substantial disciplines.

The Finnish-method has, if I am correct to make the assumption, has connected the dots between esoteric and exoteric groups and has followed the trajectory of a tale journeying from one community to another. Underlining the fluid and diffusive characteristics of tales, the Finnish school has created an international network for folklore studies, rendering the comparative studies easier and feasible to produce. The school's systematic and meticulous indices of the tale types covering a vast area of objects and themes have proved to be essential and indispensable sources for folklorists from different and even counter methodologies. Alan Dundes, for example, despite his reservations about some of the issues raised by the school, has given its due: "...the six -volume Motif-Index of Folk-Literature and the Aarne-Thompson tale type index constitute two of the most valuable tools in the professional folklorist's arsenal of aids for analysis" ("The Motif-Index and the Tale Type Index"195).

Although a thirty-year delay separates Vladimir Propp's influential work *Morphology of Folktale*'s publication in 1928 and its translation to English in 1958, its introduction to the English-speaking scholars, Propp's reputation as one of the established figures of folk literature and *Morphology*'s impact on scholars such as Alan Dundes, Claude Levi-Strauss, Claude Bremond and Algirdas Julien Greimas cannot be repudiated. Propp's taxonomic model's sphere of influence is not limited to folk literature per se, but extended to "all types of narratives be it folklore, literature, film, television series, theater, games, mimes, cartoon strips, advertisements, dance forms, sports commentaries, film theory, news reports, story generation and interactive drama systems etc" (Dogra 410). Structuralism, specifically, Claude Levi-Strauss's seminal works offered exciting opportunities for folklore studies and the divergent paths Propp and Strauss took only added to the further expansion and developments in the field. Levi-Strauss's readings, just like Propp's, found a wide coverage in numerous disciplines and subject matters, and the explanatory potential of those readings were so great to the point of eclipsing the import of the materials they undertook to study: "The beauty of structural models can become central to such studies, overshadowing the importance of the material, its creators, and the historical, cultural, and per-formative contexts from which folklore emerges" (Harle 14). The mental states of the characters and the psychological components of a tale, some of the material overlooked or outweighed by Structuralism, were taken up by Psychoanalysts, thus providing folkloristics with new horizons to navigate. Ultimately, this new horizon depended to a great extent on the unconscious, latent dynamics of a tale and the folklorists, with the tools available to them, sought to identify the traces and the links between the manifest and the hidden registers of a text.

As can be observed, despite their different and at times conflicting approaches, each methodology and school of thought progressed by building on the extant or on the preceding theoretical strands and respectively made a commitment to address and to complement the matters that were barely touched on or were left to oblivion. The current study's premise is to account for yet another hiatus the theoretical investigations chose not to acknowledge. Unable to fend off the temptation "to abandon oneself to a wondrous realm where class conflict" and sociohistorical basis "does not exist and where harmony reigns supreme" (Zipes 23), the methodologies opted to put a distance between themselves and historico-materialist, historicist interpretations of the tales in question. In fact, aside from Jack Zipes's *Breaking the Magic Spell: Radical Theories of Folk and Fairy Tales* and *Fairy Tales and the Art of Subversion: The Classical Genre for Children and the Process of Civilization*, Lutz Röhrich's influential work *Folktales and Reality* and a number of critics and literary theorists such as Michele Rak, Rudolf Schenda and Eugene Weber, the number of works and the critics dealing with the socio-political and historical bases of the folk and the fairy tales forms a small part of the whole corpus of the folklore studies. The current study's theoretical departure is historico-materialist in perspective and the overall methodological layout is structured around this pivotal point. Nevertheless, eclectic in certain respects, the methodology purports to run the gamut from history to literature, therefore numerous scholars and theorists are appropriated in drawing up its theoretical structure. Hopefully, the study will meet the challenge of delving into the mist of history with the hope of discerning the "fragments of light that come from the lost mystery" (Agamben 7). Striving to catch a few glimpses of the recondite fire in the process of writing its own *storia*, the study hopes to offer interpretations of tales that have not been deracinated from their socio-historical matrices.

Straddling History and Literature

Perhaps the best way to commence a study addressing the poles of history and literature is to retrace one's steps in time and take a look at one of the earliest proponents of historicism in literature. Giambattisto Vico, an influential philosopher and a critic of the mid-eighteenth century, propounded the idea of *modificazioni*, the potency through and in which human mind could perceive the origins of culture, the beginnings of the primary social forms and of the literary-poetic- genesis of the world. Vico insisted that no man has a nature, a natural propensity, other than history, and it is the key to understand an ancient literary work for it enables a reader or a critic to transplant his mindset to that of the author. It is crucial, for instance, to grasp the motivation behind Homer's *Iliad* or Virgil's *Aeneid* since our nature (in Vico's terminology human nature is equated with history) enables us to be in the position of both the author and the reader. Interestingly enough, Vico's historicism is not limited to individual cognition alone but encompasses quite a wide range.

> For him the world of the nations, *il mondo delle nazioni*, embraces not only political history but also the history of thought, of expression (language, literature, the fine arts), religion, law, and economics. Because all these follow from the cultural state of human society in a given period and consequently must be understood in relation to

one another or else cannot be understood at all, an insight into one of these facets of human creativity at a given stage of development must provide a key to all the others at the same age. (Auerbach 8)

For Vico, history is a cycle, sometimes a vicious one, unlike a linear progression of development and perfection, follows a course from an initial primitive epoch (the age of giants, barbarians and monsters), to a somehow golden age of heroes and social stability, and then finally descends down a primitive stage: "Thus human history and society are created through a laborious process of unfolding, development, contradiction, and, most interestingly, representation." This representation, the zeitgeist of an epoch, has its own "method, or optic, for seeing and then articulating reality" (Said xiii) and thanks to *modificazioni*, Erich Auerbach calls them "potentialities," we are able to connect ourselves with that optical, representational point and thus be able to re-examine history (a literary work) from the point of view of its author. Erich Auerbach relied to a great extent on Giambattista Vico's theories, and wrote his widely respected work *Mimesis: The Representation of Reality in Western Literature* in accordance with Vico's methodology.

Despite its Platonic, essentialist tones, its treatment of history as universal law illustrated in the ontogenesis of all nations, and its indifference to sociopolitical variants concerning the development of particular nations, Vico's and Auerbach's way of reading literature has made one significant contribution: the interconnectedness between seemingly disparate units of literature, history, economics, and religion. Positing these parts to be members not of a conflict-free, non-contradictory unity but of an entity ever unfolding with conflicts and contradictions, both Vico and Auerbach opened a new vista on looking at the representation of reality in Western literature. For some, the representation of reality in folk literature and its uses in political propaganda led to one of the most atrocious events in European history. The Brothers Grimm's collection of German folktales played an important role in building up a German national identity and which was later seized on by the Nazis and resulted in "the Nazification of the discipline"[5] Lutz Röhrich, even after the World War II, recounts that the publications by the British and the American press called for the demonization of the Grimm brothers and of the German folktales as the culprits of cruelties committed in the concentration camps.

---

5   Please see *The Nazification of an Academic Discipline: Folklore in the Third Reich* edited by James Dow and Hannjost Lixfeld.

> After the Second World War a tidal wave of press against the 'horrors of the Grimm tales appeared . . . [and] the Anglo-Saxon occupational powers temporarily forbade the printing of any new folk-tale collection because folktales made the German people cruel; folktales, they claimed, had played a major role in the developments of the methods used in the concentration camps. (Röhrich 112)

In no unclear terms, Röhrich rejects the charge that folktales acted as the instigators of violence, and counters it by a claim that violence was an undeniable fact and facet of daily life in Europe in the Middle Ages, therefore, folktales did not promote the use of violence for ultra-nationalist ideologies but in fact conveyed a historical truth, a class consciousness, that peasants and the subaltern classes were the victims, not the executioners, of such violence. In this regard, folktales reflected and documented the subjugation the underprivileged groups suffered at the hands of the feudal lords and were potentially subversive sources the powerful had to keep under their control: "Fairy tales rest on the opposition between high and low, but they are more likely to emphasize the disruption of social structure than they are to confirm sovereign power" ("Introduction" 8).

Lutz Röhrich's remark on the folktales' subversive potential is a point also taken up by Jack Zipes and he further elaborates on this issue by posing a question whether such disruptive potency was iterable, whether "in each new stage of civilization, in each new historical epoch, the symbols and configurations of the tales were endowed with new meaning, transformed, or eliminated in reaction to the needs and conflicts of the people within the social order" (Zipes *Fairy Tales* 7). On the part of the ruling groups Zipes maintains, the utopian images and themes aesthetically conceived in folk and fairy tales agitated the privileged few and they dismissed them as entertaining yet nonsensical pass time trinkets of the lower classes. In time, however, those "goose mother" stories easily discarded by the bourgeois rationality would become indispensable commodities and bring in huge revenues. The modern re-productions of certain stories, Cinderella, Snow White, Little Red Riding Hood to cite a few, have become substantial sources of profit for entrepreneurs and producers in film industry. Co-opted or not, in their traditional forms (perhaps a similar argument can be made for their modern renditions, at least from a socio-historical perspective), the folktales "nurtured their own forms of culture in opposition to that of the ruling classes and yet often reflecting the same ideology, even if from a different class perspective. . .. [in which] upper classes intermingled with lower classes" (Zipes *Breaking the Magic Spell* 8).

On the commingling of upper and lower classes and on the question of agency of the subalterns, Mikhail Bakhtin's literary term *carnivalesque* should be given some consideration. With its inverted semantics, and a vision of a topsy-turvy world, carnival laughter gives birth to a "second world," to an unofficial, counter folk culture that runs against the interests of the official discourse and of the prevailing ideology.

> In the Middle Ages folk humor existed and developed outside the official sphere of high ideology and literature, but precisely because of its unofficial existence, it was marked by exceptional radicalism, freedom, and ruthlessness. Having on the one hand forbidden laughter in every official sphere of life and ideology, the Middle Ages on the other hand between exceptional privileges of license and lawlessness outside these spheres: in the marketplace, on feast days, in festive recreational literature. And medieval laughter knew how to use these widely. (71)

Contrary to the putative view of history, that is, its teleological, linear discourse dictated by a monologic, monolithic mindset of a ruling class, the image of history invoked by folk humor is of a cyclical nature and incorporates elements that are inchoate and characterized by a diversity of voices that confirm or negate one another. For Bakhtin, the pieces for such "secondary" or "counter" image of history could be found in carnivals (in folk culture) and in literature (specifically in novel form). In the polyphony of a text or in the din of a market place, various voices or classes, from that of the peasants, fishmongers, serfs, craftsmen, and laborers to magistrates, nobles, dukes, and lords can be heard to make their demands on the totality of a narrative or on a public sphere.

Apropos of the discussions on folklore, literature, and history propounded by Giambattista Vico, Erich Auerbach, Lutz Röhrich, Jack Zipes, and Mikhail Bakhtin, despite their distinct standpoints, certain analogical arguments could be put in perspective. Concerning the use and the import of these categories, it would not be wrong to claim that the cited scholars do not treat them as isolated, thing-in-itself entities, but instead postulate them as integrated, inter-connected branches, equally important in processing and addressing the human experience. Lutz Röhrich's case above all is interesting since Röhrich endeavors to free German folktales from the grip of an ideologically driven historiography, the imputation that the tales were the *casus belli* of the WWII, and instead hopes to re-position them in materially determined historical processes. Secondly, the power of resilience, of agency is restored to subaltern groups as the producers and the conduits of folktales, and the focal point is directed on their socio-politically and historically charged deeds than on the objects or themes supposed to shape the cross-national diffusion of the tales. Lastly, also related to the second point, not only the underprivileged classes but also the privileged ones are given consideration in the analyzes and their interactions are covered not from a unilateral dichotomy of oppressor-oppressed but from a multilateral angle whereby power, in a Foucauldian twist, is disseminated through microcenters and it could be found in the very capillary structures of individual preferences. Mikhail Bakhtin's *carnivalesque* may correspond to such seam-infused power struggle as it takes into account varying and at times conflicting discourses contesting for leverage.

In fact, from the last decades of the Medieval Europe to the late period of the Renaissance, the folk was imagined to be the intimate Other, existing within the imperial, national borders of a state, "close enough both to arouse and to defile the right-thinking bourgeois individual," and simultaneously "exciting nostalgia and repudiation" (Noyes 16). With the surge of the overseas explorations beginning in the early fifteenth century up until the late seventeenth, European nations discovered not only wealth and exotic animals in the hitherto uncharted lands, but a new type of Otherness; radical, primitive, and alien. In *The Writing of History*, Michel de Certeau claims that the discovery of the indigenous subject of colonial discourse had repercussions on the historiography of Europe and on the position of the folk, the familiar yet estranged Other, in the socio-cultural milieu (44–46). The fascination with the "primitive" and archaic myths provided the historians with hermeneutical tools to write the story/history of Europe from the paradigm of difference; how Europe's history marked itself off from that of the primitive Others who were thought to live in an allochronic (not contemporaneous) time zone. Such paradigm shift had helped to pull the folk to the center of mainstream historiography, and against the recently discovered primitive Other, the folk's ancient stories were incorporated into national histories.

Edward Said's groundbreaking work *Orientalism* shed a different light on Europe's interest in the Other and studied the motives behind European imperialism when its compass pointed in the direction of the Middle East. Said maintained that literary, religious, cultural, artistic, historical, scientific and ultimately political accounts of the East rendered a representation of the Orient that was a source of nourishment for the European imagination.

> The Orient then seems to be, not an unlimited extension beyond the familiar European world, but rather a closed field, a theatrical stage affixed to Europe...In the depths of this Oriental stage stands a prodigious cultural repertoire whose individual items evoke a fabulously rich world: the Sphinx, Cleopatra, Eden, Troy, Sodom and Gomorrah, Astarte, Isis and Osiris, Sheba, Babylon, the Genii, the Magi, Nineveh, Prester John, Mahomet, and dozens more; settings, in some cases names only, half-imagined, half-known; monsters, devils, heroes; terrors, pleasures, desires. The European imagination was nourished extensively from this repertoire. (*Orientalism* 63)

The allure of the larger-than-life, legendary creatures, fairies, witches, kings, queens, princes, princesses, and laymen once sustained by "Hansel and Gretel," "Cinderella," "Snow White," "Sleeping Beauty," and "Rapunzel" was roused anew by the introduction of Oriental stories of "Aladdin's Wonderful Lamp," "Shahryar and Scheherazade," and "Ali Baba and the Forty Thieves." The incorporation of the Eastern stories into the Western tradition of folklore could be said to work both ways: as Said pointed out, the absorption of the Middle Eastern folklore into Europe might have reinforced the accounts through which European Imperialism justified its colonization of the Orient and even fortified the ostensible sense of European superiority over the Oriental identity. Or, contra Said, it can be argued that those Middle Eastern tales functioned as bridges pointing away from fixed, monolithic, and hierarchical analyzes and instead focused on the multiplicity of social identities and their interactions within culturally hybrid formations, in the "liminal space, in-between the [binary] designations of identity" (Bhabha 5).

The Ottoman Empire, an integral yet long overlooked part of the European history, has intriguingly been left out Edward Said's book and one of the criticisms raised against Said culminates on this omission. Derek Bryce sees the absence of the Ottomans as a deliberate choice on the part of Edward Said and argues that with the Ottoman Empire's rule over Anatolia, the Middle East, and the Eastern Europe for five centuries, the Empire established a unity between different nations that seemed antithetical to Said's views: "Indeed, it is the disruptive 'unity' of that Ottoman milieu, in its historical occurrence and subsequent legacy, that is 'always already' intolerable to the binary operations of Orientalism. It therefore requires constant occlusion, for specific refutation must be preceded by acknowledgment of the 'problem' of the discursive implications of Ottoman presence" (Bryce 101). In "Ottoman Orientalism," Ussama Makdisi sees Ottoman Orientalism as representations of "their own Arab periphery as an integral part of their engagement with, explicit resistance to, but also implicit acceptance of, Western representations of the indolent Ottoman East" (768). Edhem Eldem, in "The Ottoman Empire and Orientalism: An Awkward Relationship" asserts that the reason why Orientalist representations produced by the West circumvented the Ottoman Empire was due to the "familiarity of the West with the Ottomans, compared to some more remote, 'exotic,' and later discovered peoples of the East," thus making the Ottomans "less likely to attract the attention of essentialist discourses" (214). Makdisi's and Eldem's observations are apt in extending the scope of the term Orientalism and in bringing in fresh discussions on a term that is laden with diverse opinions. However, as noted by the critiques of Edward Said, a similar criticism of ahistoricity can be raised against the monolithic treatment of Eastern and Western subjectivities. One of the most well-known criticism directed against Said came from Bernard Lewis who, in his article "The Question of Orientalism," accused Said of an "arbitrary

rearrangement of the historical background" and "a capricious choice of coun-
tries, persons and writings" (112). David Kopf and John MacKenzie also took
issue with Said's approach and MacKenzie pointed out that during the eighteenth
and the nineteenth centuries, Britain's foremost Other was France not an Eastern
nation and thus found Said's account lacking in the heterogeneity and the "sheer
porousness" of imperial culture (208).

Implemented within the current discussion on the representations
of Turkish and Moorish characters in Italian folk literature, the views
propounded by Makdisi, Eldem, Lewis, Kopf and Mackenzie have their
respective uses. Although Makdisi limits his analysis of Ottoman Orientalism
to nineteenth century and does not focus on the peripheral position of the
minorities within the Ottoman Empire, his analysis is pertinent on account of
the Ottomans' engagements with the West that moved between incorporating
relevant Western values and repudiating incongruous ones. Eldem's claim
may be feasible to a certain extent, that is, "familiarity of the West with the
Ottomans" may explain the unwillingness of the West to produce essentialist
discourses on the Ottoman Empire, yet, the existence of certain texts, such
as Giovanni Battista Nazari's *Discorso sulla futura etsperata vittoria contro il
Turco*, renders Eldem's claim partially true since Ottomans were subject to
essentialist productions that labeled them as "savage," "bloodthirsty" infidels.
As a matter of fact, the Moors were tarred with the same brush reserved for
the Ottomans: "The 'Turk' was cruel and tyrannical, deviant, and deceiving;
the 'Moor' was sexually overdriven and emotionally uncontrollable, vengeful,
and religiously superstitious" (Matar 13).

What would be the implications of moving the Ottomans and the Moors into
the focus of European literature and history? Against the long-ingrained dichotomies of "Asia vs. Europe, Islam vs. Christendom, and the senselessly violent
Oriental barbarian against the thoughtfully violent Western knight" (Brummett
46), could other modalities be taken into consideration in one's approach to the
figure of the Other? Could the image of the unfamiliar Turk and the Moor be
reflected upon vis-à-vis the familiar figures, peasants, women, children, slaves,
that are traditionally relegated to the status of the Other in Italian folklore and
history?

The Other's Mirror

Mirrors as quotidian or magical objects are frequently used in folk tales and
despite their different functions for different cultures, almost every nation has
at least one tale that revolves around these phenomenal objects. The myth of

Narcissus is perhaps the most well-known story of reflective surfaces, relating the events that befell on a young man of exquisite beauty whose demise eventually takes place due to his morbid obsession with his own image. The other oft-cited tale is that of Medusa, one of the three Gorgon sisters, whose gaze would turn anyone into stone if one dared to look her in the eye. Stith Thompson's *Motif-Index of Folk-Literature* documents numerous cases of mirrors in which they sometimes operate with "clairvoyant and transforming abilities," or as "doorways to fantastic realms" (Chalupa 628). Due to the superstitious belief in their potential to cross into metaphysical realms, the mirrors were treated with caution and in Grimm's *Deutsches Worterbuch* (German Dictionary), the entry under "Spiegel" recounted the German people's fear, especially for children, of not gazing "into the mirror after dusk" and it was "advised that all reflective surfaces be covered after death to prevent the soul of the deceased from returning to haunt the living" (ibid.).

Fearsome and mysterious, the diversity of the motifs attributed to the power of the mirrors made them one of the most malleable objects in folk literature. One of those themes that was conjured here and there was the theme of the doppelgänger, a ghostly double of a living person. The examples of ghastly resemblance with the other reflected via a mirror or off the flesh of a living being can be found in certain literary works. Edgar Allan Poe's short story "William Wilson" is one of those works whose protagonist, haunted by his twin antagonist, stabs himself to death in the palace of the duke Di Broglio in Rome. Orhan Pamuk's *The White Castle* (*Beyaz Kale*) narrates a different case of the uncanny other not based on fear but on a cheerful optimism. Pamuk's novel follows the story of a young Italian scholar who is taken prisoner while sailing from Venice to Naples. He finds himself a captive of the Turkish Sultan in Istanbul and given to the service of a man called Hoja. From then on, the plot of the novel is weaved through intricate events that finally reveal the striking similarities, physical as well as spiritual, between the Italian captive and the Turkish Hoja. After a failed siege to which Hoja and his Italian companion were expected to help by their newly designed siege engine, Hoja and the scholar swap places, Hoja walks into a mist never to be seen, and the Venetian scholar, after the Sultan's pardon, assumes Hoja's place as the royal astronomer of the Topkapı Palace. In this story, Pamuk effaces the boundary between the East and the West so much so that the two the identities of the characters blend into one another to the point of indistinguishability. The gist of the novel is oriented around this theme of look-alikeness which Pamuk summarizes in the following words.

> But we should search for the strange and surprising in the world, not within ourselves!
> To search within, to think so long and hard about our own selves, would only make us
> unhappy. This is what had happened to the characters in my story: for this reason heroes
> could never tolerate being themselves, for this reason they always wanted to be someone
> else. (154–155)

The process of becoming something or someone other than who one is may
harbor instances of mutual goodwill as Pamuk's novel indicates, yet there are
other instances in which the mirror and the reflections it projects do not bode
well, as is the case with "William Wilson" or "Narcissus," and are prone to
complications. Marina Formica's *Lo specchio turco: Immagini dell'altro e riflessi
del sé nella cultura italiana d'età moderna* (*The Turkish Mirror: Images of the Other
and Reflections of the Self in Modern Italian Culture*) provides one such complex interpretation of the Ottoman counterpart to Italian national identity and
she explores the connotations (junctions and the vicissitudes) of the Ottoman
identity for those populations thought to constitute the highest echelons and
the lowest dregs of the Italian society. Formica argues that the Turkish identity
became the Other par excellence for Europe and the Italian society between the
fifteenth and the eighteenth centuries and acting in the capacity of a mirror, Turks
reflected "delle paure e delle angosce, delle qualità e dei difetti della cristianità
occidentale" ("the fears and anxieties, of the qualities and defects of Western
Christianity") (Formica 4). This mirror, for Formica, was useful at times for the
crisis and the traumas the Italian society experienced during the given centuries
since the Turkish Other functioned as the enemy and the alter ego of the nation
unifying its populations around the images of a scapegoat or of a second self.

> Incapace a risolvere quei traumi provocati sia dal confronto con l'esterno (l'America
> e l'Eccelsa Porta appunto), sia, e soprattutto, dal rapporto non risolto con le proprie
> molteplici lacerazioni interne (le spinte riformatrici, il moltiplicarsi di posizioni e
> gruppi eterodossi o radicali), la cultura occidentale, in ispecie nei momenti di mag-
> giore difficoltà religiosa, economica, militare, sociale, rappresentò l'Ottomano sia
> come nemico sia come alter ego, in positivo e in negativo, all'interno di un complesso
> processo volto a recuperare, accentuandoli, i propri tratti accomunanti, le ragioni di
> un'appartenenza ora esplicitamente criticata ora posta in discussion. (ibid.)

> Unable to resolve those traumas caused by the confrontation with the outside world and,
> above all, by the unresolved relationship with its many internal conflicts (the pressures
> for reform, the multiplication of positions and the presence of the heterodox or rad-
> ical groups), Western culture, especially in the moments of greatest religious, economic,
> military, social difficulty, represented the Ottoman both as an enemy and as an alter ego,
> in positive and negative forms, within a complex process aimed at recovering, by accen-
> tuating them, their common features, the reasons for a membership explicitly criticized,
> and questioned.

The Ottomans in Formica's book could be said to comprise mirror function that is tantamount to plane surface of reflection in regards to projecting the fears, anxieties, and the desires of the Italians that eventually shaped the Italian identity vis-à-vis the Ottoman other. The interactions as Formica points out were convoluted, if a war was being waged against the Turkish armies, the Turks were represented as the fiendish, infidel enemy of the nation or when the internal divisions ravaged the country and thus had to be kept under control, Turks were given as the epitome of fidelity and submissiveness to authority. In this vein, the Ottoman identity cemented the bondage between different groups in Italy and from the fifteenth to the eighteenth century, the Ottoman Other paved the way for a united Italian national identity (Formica 5).

As a matter of fact, between the fifteenth and the eighteenth centuries, the Ottoman-Italian relations vacillated between discord and accord and a few landmark events brought these two nations together in bad blood and good will. The fall of Constantinople in 1453 to Sultan Mehmed, the brief occupation of Otranto by the Ottomans in 1480, the allocation of a thirteenth century palazzo to Turkish merchants in 1621 as a bona fide token of the Venetians, the Treaty of Constantinople signed in 1479, granting trade concessions to the Republic of Venice, and the battle of Lepanto uniting Christian Europe against the "infidel" Muslim Turks have undeniably left indelible marks on the imagination of the Italian people and given vent to their fantasies about the exotic stranger or to their fears about the heinous outsider. The ruling classes truly took advantage of the long drawn scuffles between the two nations and consciously or unconsciously planted the first germs of nationhood among their respective subjects/ citizens that later blossomed into somehow stable national identities. Placing the folktales at the center of analysis, the tales that deal with the Other (Muslim/ Asian/African/Turkic) would, hopefully, furnish us not only with the macro socio-political modalities but also with the micro realities that prove to be more complex than anticipated.

In the introduction to his collection of *Italian Folktales*, Italo Calvino draws attention to distinct sociopolitical systems and relations constituting the separate class-oriented backgrounds for the Western and the Eastern folktales.

> The folktale clothes its motifs in the habits of diverse societies. In the West the imprint of feudalism prevailed (notwithstanding certain nineteenth-century touches in the south such as an English lord) while in the Orient the bourgeois folktale of the fortunes of Aladdin or of Ali Baba dominated." (xxviii)

Nevertheless, Calvino also adds that "folktales are the same the world over," in regards to their encompassing the essentialist and arbitrary divisions of human beings into "kings and poor people" and in this particular sense he further posits that "folktales are real" (xviii–xix). Regarding the division of human beings along socioeconomic lines, some functional similarities could be identified in Italian and Turkish folktales. Baciccin Tribordo (known as Samphire Starboard in English translation) in "L'uomo verde d'alghe" ("The Man Wreathed in Seaweed") tale and Keloğlan (The Bald Boy) can be compared in view of their struggles for a just social order. What Baciccin Tribordo and Keloğlan initially bring to the sociocultural milieus of their nations is the sense of justice that is not meted out by the state, but justice set aright and earned by those who are wronged in the first place. Secondly, the characters embody the hope that even the discarded, rank and file strata of the society (Baciccin a vagabond, and an inveterate drunkard and Keloğlan a desperately poor and a lazy figure) could climb up the ladder of social recognition, in a manner of pulling oneself up by one's bootstraps and would eventually be rewarded. The reward may be obtained on account of one or of combination of numerous factors: bravery, pure chance, cunning, wisdom and moral uprightness. In the two tales, we see various functions coming into play, but what is foregrounded is the issue of morality, perhaps more vital and significant in an anomic society. Occupying the position of the Other in their respective communities, Baciccin and Keloğlan demonstrate that there is a crack in the plane mirror of the society and something awry in the images it casts back on its members. A comparable and a complementary argument of Otherness that joins an Italian and an "exotic" other together could be made for Giraldi Cinthio's "The Moor of Venice."

The short story, which for some was the inspiration behind William Shakespeare's famous play *Othello*, recounts the great love between the Moorish general and Disdemona, the daughter of a noble Venetian family. The plot is a well-known one, Shakespeare's *Othello* also follows a similar story line, that the Moor is duped into believing in the infidelity of his wife by the evil Ensign, and with the help of this wicked man, the Moor has the Captain (the supposed lover) and Disdemona killed. At times the story drops hints as to the racial Otherness of the Moor and to his "natural" tendency to anger: "Nay, but you Moors are of so hot a nature that every little trifle moves you to anger and revenge" (Cinthio 4). In another case, once again uttered by Disdemona, the cultural and the racial gap between Italians and Moors is stressed: "I shall prove a warning to young girls not to marry against the wishes of their parents, and that the Italian ladies may learn from me not to wed a man whom nature and habitude of life estrange from us" (Cinthio 8). The admonition put into the mouth of Disdemona can be claimed to attest to the prevailing fear of miscegenation, to the anxieties centered on race-sex nexus. Similar to Marica Formica's ideas on Ottomans and the subaltern groups in Italy, Luigi Lombardi Satriani asserts that alterity has been co-opted to uphold the hierarchical organizations in a society and to help sustain the so-called normative categories delineated by a privileged faction.

> Storicamente altre sono apparse come se fossero ontologicamente altre: il primitivo, il nero, l'ebreo, la donna, l'omosessuale, con varietà di accenti, ma con uguale sistematicità, hanno rappresentato l'ambito di realizzazione della tensione gerarchizzante delle società o, meglio, di quella parte della società che si è autoeletta punto di riferimento e custode assoluta dell'identità-umanità-normalità. (63)

> Historically others appeared as if they were ontologically other: the primitive, the black, the Jew, the woman, the homosexual, with a variety of accents, but with equal systematicity, represented the sphere of realization of the hierarchical tension of societies or, better, of that part of society that has elected itself as a reference point and absolute guardian of identity-humanity-normality.

Pierre Macherey believes that a book's manifest registers of meaning are always accompanied by a "certain absence," by a tacitly implied, latent silence. The fact that a book does not give voice to certain things and prefers to leave them in the shadows of the text does not diminish the significance of the hidden content for "in order to say anything, there are other things which must not be said" (85). This unacknowledged silence tells us something nevertheless, a meta-meaning if you will, informing us "of the precise conditions for the appearance of an utterance, and thus its limits" (86). In its methodology, the current study will follow a somewhat analogous trajectory to that of Macherey and will closely read both the articulated, fully worked-out meanings and the inferred, between the lines signifying processes in the selected tales. Effectuating an alternate reality that reveals the illusory integrity of a society, and pointing out to the raging contradictions running free beneath the surface appearance of calm and consonant subjectivities, the Italian folktales will be addressed from a mutually imbricated context of history and literature. Positioned at tangent, counter, or slanting angles to the ruling groups, the folktales of Italy are read in the capacity of a syncretic form of social *heteroglossia* characterized by the interplay of several voices. It is contended that the Ottoman and the Moorish Others in Italian folk literature play significant roles in struggles for power as conduits for subjugation or as props to counter the official conceptions. Mediating the discordant and incompatible social realities and functioning as anchor points preserving the delicate equilibrium of hegemonic alliances or symbolic lapses mirroring the fears, anguishes, and the defects of the Italian nation, the convoluted tales of Italians, Turks, and Moors will be given in the subsequent chapters.

II. Turks in Italian Folktales

The Legend of Balaban the Janissary

In the small Italian village of Moena of Trento region, a story of the utmost curiosity and mystery is being told. The inhabitants of this Alpine town organize and celebrate the annual *Festa di Turchia* in the second week of July in memory of a janissary who happened to settle in the village after a series of unlikely events. The legend has it that during the second siege of Vienna by the Ottoman Empire in 1683, a wounded soldier of the Sultan's army runs for his life and arrives in a village on the foothills of Manzori mountains. The villagers, instead of capturing or executing the Turkish deserter, tend to his wounds, allow him to stay and even let him marry a girl from the town. While adapting to the local customs, the janissary also begins to exert his influence on the community especially after his heroic stand against the tyrannical rule of the Duchy of Augsburg. Well versed in martial arts, the janissary, or Il Turco as he was called by the locals, teaches the villagers how to make bows and arrows, trains them on swordfight and on the use of firearms, thus Il Turco gives them the courage to fight against the heavy taxation and the cruel dominion of the feudal lords. Following such feat of bravery, locals have come to revere this foreigner from a distant land, and to this day, his memory is cherished and blended in the communal lore. In the Turkish version of the story, one can get the missing link of the tale, that is, Il Turco's deeds during the siege of Vienna, and a different portrayal of the protagonist as the Turkish sources[6] claim that the janissary is no ordinary soldier and that he is a well learned and trained high ranking officer with a name. Balaban Hasan (Il Turco) is crucial for the Grand Vizier Kara Mustafa Pasha's schemes for the fall of Vienna, yet, Balaban is a rebellious soul and he takes a stand against the Pasha for the delay of the decisive assault on the castle and the city walls. Obviously, such daring criticism against the second man of the empire has its consequences, and Balaban is sentenced to death. Taking pity on their comrade's fate, and probably sharing his resentment, janissaries help him escape, and the rest of his story is weaved as narrated by the people of Moena.

The story of Il Turco and the festival that has been an integral part of Moena identity for 335 years have received little attention from historians and men of

---

6   Please see Orhan Kologlu's *"Ceriale' nin İtalyan Türkleri"* (2004) and Ermanno Visintainer's "La Presenza Turca Dimenticata In Italia: I Turchi Di Moena" (2011).

letters, perhaps, on account of its supposed singularity and of its assumed his-
toriographic insignificance. Or, the reason could further be attributed to a general
tendency of the Renaissance scholars who often referred to clash of civilizations
thesis[7] while addressing the interactions between Muslim Turks and Christian
Europe and thus opted for a "settled certainties about European 'progress' in
the face of eastern 'stagnation' or 'decline'" (MacLean, 21). Such oppositional
pairs, "Asia vs. Europe, Islam vs. Christendom, the senselessly violent Oriental
barbarian against the thoughtfully violent Western knight" (Brummett 46), were
consciously crafted dichotomies, drawing their inspiration from biased political
accounts and fantasy laden literary works produced during the fifteenth and the
sixteenth centuries. In fact, one can argue that despite their differences in tones
and contexts, political reports and literary works overlapped and complemented
one another in creating tropes that portrayed Turks as exoteric and at times
exotic enemies of Christendom. One such example, the *Discorso sulla futura et
sperata vittoria contro il Turco*, penned by Giovanni Battista Nazari in 1570, featured mythological creatures representing the Holy League and the Ottomans
clashing in Lepanto. The book depicted the imperial eagle, the papal lamb, and
the Venetian lion attacking the crescent bearing Turkish dragon and, with the
help of the mighty god, their eventual victory over this nemesis of freedom.
Some dispatches (relazioni) sent by the Venetian ambassadors posted in Istanbul
followed a similar trajectory to that of Nazari and combined political propaganda with fictional accounts. A certain ambassador by the name of Ottaviano
Bon delivered a report on the confidential life in Sultan's harem, claiming to have
sneaked into the seraglio while Sultan was away. A report based on observation, hearsay and fantasy, the dispatch had customers, and still has as the English
translation is in its third print, and provided a "political and sexual" voyeurism
for its readers. Despite their confidential status, relazioni were leaked now and
then, and the "proliferation of different versions" and "the many different uses
to which various people put these texts" generated a literary circle of authorship
and readership whereby people adopted some of the official viewpoints on the
Ottomans (De Vivo 30). Expressions such as "I saw the Sultan of Turkey, who
bought himself twenty new wives" (Calvino 55) in "The Canary Prince" tale from
the region of Piedmont, or "Even if you have two wives instead of one, so what?

---

7   Bernard Lewis and later Samuel Huntington who envisaged an eternal and relent-
     less battle between the Judeo-Christian west and the Islamic east popularized the
     Manichean view that divided the world history between two mutually exclusive
     civilizations.

The Turks have as many as twelve" (Calvino 248) in "The King of Portugal's Son" from the province of Pistoia in the Tuscany region point to such transitions from official discourse to a popular one, received and accepted without modifications.

Notwithstanding the coinciding themes that subsequently etched in Italian public opinion and popular imagination the figures of "menacing" and "lustful" Turk, fabular representations, as is the case with the Moena story of Il Turco, also pointed away from the official accounts and introduced their unique and alternative mapping (Calvino xxviii). In Luigi Lombardi-Satriani's words, Italian folk culture marked the "outer limit of the hegemonic culture," revealed its "ideological tricks," and contested "the universality. . .of the official culture's concepts of the world and life" (Lombardi-Satriani 104). Combining history and literature, and drawing on Antonio Gramsci's notion of hegemony and Claude Levi-Strauss' structural model, the present chapter contends that the selected Italian folktales present a site of contestation in which several class positions and discourses vie with one another for ascendancy, and it is maintained that in such theater of power the Turkish characters are assigned roles that either support the *status quo* or undermine the authority of a hegemonic order or mediate dissensions between a regime and its subjects. It is argued that such line of inquiry and interpretation would depart from settled certainties about the enduring conflicts between East and West and would instead provide a dynamic reading in which cultural exchanges between these two nations take place in reciprocal rather than univocal histories, and on porous, non-rigid political and imaginary borderlands.

The Winding Paths of Hegemony and Identity

In certain respects, Gramsci's thoughts on folk culture and literature were not far from Karl Marx's sack of potatoes analogy. Marx regarded peasants not as a class but as "homologous magnitudes," living in close quarters and self-sufficient material conditions with parochial, backward, and reactionary dispositions. Incapable of "asserting their rights in their own name," peasants were small, insular groups who could not represent themselves but had to be represented by an authority through whom they sought protection from other classes and even awaited "rain and sunshine from above" (85). On the subject of a regressive mindset, and the subaltern status, Gramsci shared Marx's views, specifically on how "folklore has always been tied to the culture of the dominant class and, in its own way, has drawn from it the motifs which have then become inserted into combinations with the previous traditions" (194). Besides such "fossilized," "conservative," and "reactionary" layer, this is where he parts ways with

Marx, Gramsci also saw an oppositional, therefore a subversive potential in folklore. Containing strata of archaic and modern "conceptions of the world and life," folklore had a revolutionary energy that needed to be revealed by a counterhegemonic consciousness for "hegemony. . .attends to consciousness, to ways of thinking" (Gencarella 222). The contestation played out on the level of consciousness between the dominator and the dominated, however, was not unilateral and marked by impermeable borders:

> . . .the world of the dominated and that of the dominators are not monolithically contraposed, with only one point of contact through which domination is exercised. Instead, they live in strict, daily contact, themes from the dominated culture mixing with themes from the hegemonic culture, and some of these latter passing into the subordinate (or folk) culture. (Satriani 107)

A few examples of transitions of official themes (without modifications) to subaltern lore have been mentioned in the preceding pages in passing. I think it would be pertinent to give a detailed analysis of a folktale which echoes a dominant view of the Turks and to a certain extent supports the cultural forms of the classes in power. Still, the appropriation does not exhaust the story's seditious character as the plot makes a mocking use of the cultural paradigms attributed to and by the ruling classes. The "Science of Laziness" story is from Trieste, a city that struggled for independence from the yoke of Venice but eventually placed itself under the rule of the Habsburg Empire. Though Ottomans never invaded the city, their presence was felt on the outskirts of the town as they torched the village of Prosseco on their way to capture Friuli. Whether the "lazy Turk" trope[8] was a recent invention following the pillage of Prosseco, or it was a long-ingrained stereotype in the local culture of Trieste would at best prove to be too shallow remarks to expand on. Instead, the trope that constitutes the focal point of the tale should be addressed in terms of the hegemonic relations that include the commune of Trieste, the Republic of Venice and the Ottoman Empire.

---

8   Emil Laveley, quoted in Hana Sobotková's "The Image of Balkan Muslims in Czech and French Journals around 1900" drew attention to social hierarchies found between Ottoman elites and rural Turkish populations. For Laveley, guided by his politically charged convictions, the higher ranks in the Ottoman society were "lazy, jealous, and sensuous, conservative Muslim(s) who could not bear enlightenment, innovation, and progress" while, by contrast, the lower strata despite their "oriental backwardness," were comprised of good, honest souls (Laveley quoted in Sobotková, 345). The "lazy Turk" image in the folktale may pertain to such negative traits attributed to the upper echelons of the Ottoman society.

The tale is about an old Turkish man and his son who visit a professor to learn "the science of laziness." The professor known for his indolent life welcomes the son and the father while reclining under a fig tree and he stirs occasionally to eat the ripe figs that fall down on the spot he reclines. No sooner the father begins to explain the reason for their visit than the professor cuts him short and responds ". . .don't talk so much. It tires me to listen to you. If you want to bring up your son to be a true Turk, just send him to me" (Calvino 137). Upon hearing the lackadaisical tone, the old man decides that the tutor is the man he wants and leaves the son to his custody. Endowed with a natal talent for idleness, the son lays next to his teacher and waits for a fig to come his way. Yet, instead of reaching for the fruit as his tutor does, he opens his mouth and prays for one to hit the mark. Seeing his pupil already an expert in the art of laziness, the professor sends him back to his father with the following commendation "Go home. You have nothing to learn. You can even teach me something" (Calvino 138).

Engaging with an ages-old stereotype frequently employed to label other races, ethnicities, and peoples with lower social status, the tale could be said to utilize the theme of laziness through displacement. As mentioned before, a folktale can reinforce the paradigms fostered by the ruling ideology and one can observe the quintessential instance of such support in the tale. Just like other oversimplified and exaggerated generalizations regarding the Turks, "evil," "savage," "promiscuous" etc., the stereotype of laziness harks back to an official discourse, however, whose discourse is transmitted in this particular tale is a quite controversial issue. Dodging a sack at the hands of the Ottomans in 1470, Trieste was demolished in 1468 by Holy Roman Emperor Fredrick III. The city was not also on good terms with the Venetians as the Republic sought to establish its dominion over the city and turn it into one of its vassal states. Habsburgs were lesser of two evils and like a drowning man would clutch at a straw, Trieste accepted their protection and rule. As these greater powers had negative connotations in varying degrees, it would not be wrong to look for the provenance of the trope amidst the cultural paradigms of the city itself. A motto of an aristocrat family of Trieste would bear testimony to the situation and encapsulate it much better than I have attempted to sketch above: "Italia non posso essere; Austria non voglio, Trieste con sue provincie, sono" (Pizzi 37). In essence, a unique identity of *triestinita* was an invention of the local political elites who, in their attempt to link their family lineage to the legendary Roman genealogies, introduced a "superiority complex" resulting in the creation of an inferior-outsider typology in literature (Pizzi 48).

If the overall structure of the tale is taken into account, one can catch a few glimpses of this complex and see that it differs widely from other folktales in respect to its morphological characteristics. In the story, no hero or heroine leaves his/her home or is abducted while tending to daily chores, or faces obstacles set by a malignant force. Moreover, there is no cathartic resolution through which certain ethical dilemmas or problems are amended thanks to the punishment of evil and the hero is rewarded for his/her righteous and heroic actions. In this respect, the tale "Science of Laziness" resembles more to an ethnic joke where the main idea is shaped around the exaltation of an ethnicity at the expense of belittling another national identity. This, however, is not the case with the "Science of Laziness" tale as it offers more than catches the eye. Indeed, it plays into the hands of Trieste elites by upholding the *triestinita* ideal and thus helps construct an esoteric group identity marked by the imaginary and the actual borders of the city. However, if one lends an ear to Slavoj Zizek's remark about the role of ethnic jokes in a given political milieu, an alternative reading of the "Science of Laziness" can be reached. A vulgar joke, for Zizek, disrupts the seemingly contradiction-free, serene and politically correct countenance of power and attacks not the racial, or the ethnic group that stands at the center of the disparaging joke but the subject matter that gives form to the joke itself (*Žižek's Jokes*). To take it a step further, a joke's offensive stance is in essence a confrontation with a power structure that organizes a society in accordance with hierarchical parameters of merit. The image of the lazy Turk, whose "greatest scourge on earth. . .is work," could be a negative trait attributed to the lower classes of Trieste by the upper echelons and the practice of sending wealthy adolescents to private tutors or hiring professionals for the affluent youth could be taken as a cultural routine of the gentlefolk of the city.

Introducing another folktale from a rival region which also capitalizes on Turkish characters would provide us with a better chance to address the power dynamics of Trieste at the time and allow us for further inquiry into the similar and different roles fashioned for the characters. The history of the region of Istria, now part of Croatia, somewhat followed a similar if not the same trajectory of events as that of Trieste for the region whetted the appetites of the three great powers in the sixteenth century. As has been formerly noted, Trieste chose the rule of Austrians against the monopoly of Venice whereas Istria sided with the Republic to deter its northern neighbor from expanding its borders (Darovec 39). While the life on the political stage was instable, everyday reality was beset by a severe poverty, "with no political identity of its own, yet suffering from the military incursions of three of what had become the Great Powers of their time [Venice, Austria, and the Ottoman Empire]," and the region was "frequently devastated and its people, already occupying a territory where life is always hard, were often reduced to conditions of appaling poverty and pestilence" (Unger 590). Venetians and Austrians fought over almost every patch of land no matter

how small, and even over olive groves and vineyards that had no substantial economic yields. Ideological in nature, these subterfuges left the populations of the
region in a quagmire of allegiances that further worsened the living conditions of
the communities. However, the only time these two great powers and the Istrian
communities collaborated was during the Turkish incursions into the region.
Forming a unified front against the invading enemy, the defenders were able to
fend off the Turkish attacks and thwart the attempts to seize the coastal cities of
Istria. Despite saving the urban centers from ruin, Istrians could not stop the
pillage and the plunder of the countryside and the ensuing memory of suffering
was painted in the frescoes of the church of Hrastovlje (Darovec 52).

In the sixteenth and the seventeenth centuries, the ethnic composition of Istria
was far from being homogeneous and monolingual. Consisting of Slavs, Karni,
Friulans, Italians and later Albanians and Bosnians, the region was a medley
of different cultures, nevertheless, an overarching Istrian culture, defined and
determined by the geopolitical borders of the region, constituted the main frame
of reference for cultural and social belonging. Istrians, those inhabited the peninsula long ago, regarded the recent settlers as *foresti* ("outsiders") "and in this
way kept them away from important events, forcing them to accept even more
promptly the traditional usages and customs" (ibid.). Though displaying eth-
nological unity now and then, Istran society was divided along socioeconomic
lines. Those lived in the cities, on the coast of the region, were occupied with
commerce and trade and constituted the wealthy classes of the region with ties
to the Venetian cadre of administrators, whereas those lived in the rural areas
were simple farmers who would carry "rain, dried meat, skins, wood, metals"
to the cities and would bear the brunt of raids and plagues that would torch the
countryside. The polity of the cities, based on the Venetian model, was oligarchy,
conferring power on few prosperous and prominent families, excluding the pos-
sibility of representation of the populace in the government. In this respect, compared to Trieste, Istria had no nobility that reached out to the rest of the society
and the nobility, unlike its counterpart in Trieste, was not interested in creating
a local or a regional sense of affiliation.

The folktale "Fair Brow," just like "Science of Laziness," commences with a
father and a son. The father, now that the son has finished his school, advises
his offspring to set sail and learn the skill of trade to earn his living. Being a
man of power and of means, he furnishes the son with a ship, provisions for
the journey, and with seven thousand crowns for the purchase of goods. After
sailing for a while without buying anything, the boy comes into a port and sees
a coffin on the shore in which the onlookers toss a coin. Upon asking the reason
why the body of the unfortunate man is not buried, he receives the answer that

the man passed away without paying his debts and he would not be put in the
ground until his debtors are reimbursed by the charity. Taking pity on the poor
soul, he announces to reimburse the creditors and demands the dead man to be
taken away and buried at once. Left penniless, he sails back home to his father
and makes up a story about pirates' robbing him of the allowance. The father
gives credence to the story, refunds the son with another seven thousand crowns
and gives him his blessings for the next voyage. On his second venture, the son
encounters Turkish pirates carrying on board the beautiful daughter of the
Turkish Sultan. He requests to see the legendary beauty of the maiden on account of which she is kidnapped from his father's palace, and he falls in love the
moment he lays his eyes upon her fair complexion. Buying her freedom from the
pirates for the sum of seven thousand crows, he rushes back to his father antici-
pating a warm welcome and his assent for their marriage:

> "Father, I bring a most precious gem,
> You will sing with *joy* when you see her!
> A maiden lovelier than you've e'er beheld:
> The daughter of the sultan of Turkey
> I bring as my first commodity!"

(Calvino 139)

Instead, the father meets the son with anger and insults, calling him idiot to
return home with such worthless prize and throws them in the street. No roof
over their heads and no money in their pockets, the young couple searches for a
way out of their misery. The Sultan's daughter allays her husband's anxiety a little
by informing him of her talent in painting fine pictures. If they could sell some
of those paintings, they would eke out a living for themselves. But, she adds, he
is not to tell anyone that she is the painter. Listening to his wife's counsel, the
husband approves of her plan and begins to sell the paintings in the town square.
Meanwhile, back in Istanbul, the sultan dispatches ships after ships to retrieve his
beloved daughter, probably for a handsome amount of prize money. Eventually,
his search campaign bears fruit and a detachment of Turkish soldiers approaches
the young man in the town square, immediately recognizing the hand which
painted the pictures. The young man, pleased with the interest of his customers,
offers to take them home where they can see the entire gallery and meet the artist
behind these works. Upon their arrival, the soldiers lose no time and seize the
princess and carry her back to Istanbul. After this harrowing event, the hapless
son and the husband, without money, trade and wife, strolls to the harbor every
day to find a ship to accept him on board, but as his luck is already dwindling,

he keeps getting rejected by everyone except for an old man who admits him into his small boat. Agreeing to help the young man in his hopes of retrieving his wife, the old man directs the boat to the shores of Istanbul. Before setting their feet on the ground though, their boat is captured by the Turks and the two men are fettered and brought before the Sultan. Enslaving them, the Sultan puts them to work in the palace garden. Now the young man Fair Brow, as his wife calls him by that affectionate alias, has a beautiful voice and he sings when not tending to the royal garden. Chance has it that one day his songs fall upon the ears of the princess and the lovers are thus re-united. They eventually escape with a considerable sum of the Turkish treasury but Fair Brow remembers his friend the old man, returns to the shore and saves him from the grip of slavery. The old man turns out to be soul of the dead man for whose burial Fair Brow has paid and thus all good luck stems from that good deed. Being the richest nobleman on earth, Fair Brow and his wife are welcomed back to the city harbor with cannon fires and "who should be waiting on shore with open arms but his father" (Calvino 141).

In *Italian Popular Tales*, the story "Fair Brow" is listed under the fairy tales category, yet the collector Thomas Frederick Crane also claims that the tale could be included in the legends as it contains characteristics that could be attributed to both groups. For the former classification, the tale is built on some of the major themes of fairy tales, that is, the themes of love, separation and reunion. As for the legends class, it encompasses an old theme of "the thankful dead" in which the hero or the heroine is rewarded for its good actions towards the dead. Crane maintains that the latter theme is the focal point of the story to which other episodes are secondary in significance. If one scratches the surface of the theme of "the thankful dead," one can also observe that this main incident is also a stand in for the ethical dilemmas the Istrian nobility faces at the time. Indeed, one can extend the scope of the dilemmas to the rest of the tale as it is freighted with elements that take on the subject of moral scruples whose com-pass, according to the subaltern class, has gone in the direction of wrong actions. Take the example of the rich father who has no concern for his son's emotions and morally right actions but who cares instead for the return of a good profit for his investment in his son's future. He views the bride as a worthless com-modity and rejoices only when the son returns with a ship loaded with golds and gems of utmost value. In this respect, the father is a typical figure of the selfish, hardhearted merchant of the coastline Istria, ruthlessly exploiting the inland parts of the region and bent on putting the self-interests of the family before any other worries that ail the socioeconomically handicapped populations. The son, on the other hand, is a philanthropic representative of the wealthy class as he conscientiously distributes the capital his family owns, suffers on account of his fair treatment and is eventually granted with the greatest riches of the world.

For Antonio Gramsci, the class at the helm of power seeks to establish and then preserve the delicate equilibrium of hegemonic relations by exercising a balanced authority based on *dominio* (coercion) and *direzione* (consensus). If things start to go wrong on the economic or on the ethico-political planes, coercion and/or consensus are implemented until a desired degree of stability, parallel to the interests of the dominant class, is achieved. In coercive measures, authority is imposed by brute force while in consensus, power is expected to be performed by manufacturing consent. On economic and ethico-political matters, the group dictating hegemony introduces reformative acts that would bring about not the abolishment of existing relations of domination but the redefinition of the prevailing hierarchical positions in tandem with the changing conditions in a society (Gramsci *Selected Writings*). From this standpoint, Fair Brow and his father represent two poles of the dominant class wherein legitimacy of their rule is first questioned on account of the latter's unethical stance, but later secured thanks to the former's benevolent approach towards the subaltern classes. In other words, without changing the hierarchical parameters of the society (the son, the father and the wife still constitute the wealthy class at the end of the story), Fair Brow manages to restore the consent of the subaltern classes by stopping the decadence into which the society falls. As the "grateful dead" trope forms the main point of reference for moral issues, Fair Brow's whole journey can be taken as a quest of ethics strewn with other tropes of ordeal and deliverance that befall on noblemen and peasants alike. From "crossing the threshold" of the security of his house and country in search of a better life, to "fall on hard times" to make ends meet, from "captivity" and "forced labor" to "emancipation" and "reward," the journey takes the young hero through various phases of moral tests, eventually culminating in a parable of charity and goodwill.

As for the presence of the Turkish characters in the tale, two claims can be put forward regarding their roles in shaping or sustaining such moral quest Fair Brow undertakes. First, they constitute the passive backdrop, rather the subplot, of the main narrative wherein the actions of the protagonist are interlaced with one another. To explicate it in Barthes's functions and indices, the first and the second encounters with the Turks fill in the gap between two "cardinal functions" or "nuclei" of the story; between the themes of embarking on a journey and termination of a journey, between tension and resolution (Barthes 248). The Turkish pirates provide the young nobleman with the opportunity to traverse these two main moments as he journeys back to his home with the most precious "commodity," his beautiful wife, and another group of Turkish men,

Sultan's soldiers, urges him to continue the journey. In Barthes's words once again, these encounters effectuate the function of catalyzer, giving the story its chronological order of consecution and consequence. Speaking of chronology, it behooves me to put in a few words from Mikhael Bakhtin and his views on the use of time in ancient narratives so as to expand on the function of the Turkish characters in their contribution to the "Fair Brow" tale. For Bakhtin, the action of a story unfolds on a temporal base of contingency and chance encounters of "suddenlys" and "at just that moments," without which "there would be no plot at all" (Bakhtin *The Dialogic Imagination* 92). Two chance encounters with the Turks, first the pirates then the Sultan's soldiers, furnish the tale with what it needs: imparting motion to the action(s) of the protagonist and providing "an opening for the intrusion of nonhuman forces" (ibid.). The "intrusion of non-human forces," in the case of the Fair Brow, is the appearance of the soul of the dead man who helps the hero not only to retrieve his wife but also to come into possession of a great fortune.

The second, more central role the Turkish characters have in the story, as befitting their rank, concerns the main theme of the tale, that is, the question of doing what is equitable. The agnomen Fair Brow, which also titles the tale, is given to the hero by his wife, the Turkish princess. We can surmise that in the initial stages of the story, fairness is related to a physical feature of the character but it takes on a more dignified meaning as the story progresses. The latter meaning is bestowed only after he displays acts that deserve the entitlement of just and righteous. In fact, in the Middle Ages, beauty and virtue were two terms that formed the flip sides of the same coin. Umberto Eco, in *History of Beauty*, included a few excerpts from Malleus Maleficarum (the infamous manual for witch hunters) which associated the "malice" of the witches with their lustful, thus flawed characters (Eco 2011).[9] Istrians, according to Janez Vajkard Valvasor,

---

9   Physical form and facial features have long been associated with certain "inherent" character traits that would position the subject higher or lower on the social ladder of recognition. Creating inequalities in terms of gender, the phenomena of beauty and ugliness have also been employed to create racial and even ethnic discriminations upholding the agenda of an ideology that would deploy itself as exceptional and thus superior. Please see Maxine Leeds Craig's "Race, Beauty, and the Tangled Knot of a Guilty Pleasure" (2006). Accepted into their parameters of beauty, it may be speculated that the Istrians treated the Turkish princess as an outsider who was on a par with the Istrian nobility and thanks to her, and contrary to the official discourses on Turks being the arch enemy, they came to regard the Ottomans as potential partners in trade and in marital bonds.

had similar fears and views of sorcerers, and apparitions who, they imagined, would cast their spell on poor, innocent souls of the peasants, and sneak into houses and sleep with their wives and taking their leave unnoticed (Valvasor qtd. in Darovec, 58). The Turkish princess, for her beauty, chaste, and "wifely" ways (she supports her husband in troubled times and refuses the great wealth of the father for her love) does not fit in the category of "witches" Istrians reserved for socioculturally deviant female types. In this respect, the Turkish characters hold a significant place in the tale, specifically, in complementing and augmenting the positive traits of the main character and in sustaining the underlying message of the story.

Domesticating the Enemy

As one moves to the south of Italy, it is possible to trace a more conspicuous Turkish presence as the region was a theater of war for the Ottoman Empire and the city states backed by the papacy. Before the Ottomans, Arab armies set foot on the southern tip of the peninsula and established emirates (states ruled by Arab governors) in Bari and Sicily that respectively lasted for 25 and 126 years. The consequences of the considerably long occupation turned out to be both good and bad for the occupiers and the occupied alike. On the positive side, the island of Sicily added another layer of cultural richness to its already wealthy history of multiculturalism for the Islamic civilization at the time, in Gaetano Cipolla's words, ". . .was the most advanced in the world," and the island "became the meeting point between East and West, Europe and Africa" (24). Sociopolitically, the Arab rulers introduced land reforms and thus put a dent in the protracted practice of latifundia economy which allowed for a monopoliza-tion of huge tracks of arable lands by a handful of feudal lords. On the downside, agricultural improvements made by the Arab emirs left the existing relations of production based on exploitation intact, and even placed a further load on non-Muslim inhabitants who were made to pay *jizya*, tax levied on Christians and Jews as a reminder of their inferior status. The Muslim governors were expelled from Sicily by the Normans in 1091, the Normans left their seats of power to the Spaniards in the fifteenth century, and it was during this period that the island came into contact with the Ottomans.

Though the Ottomans' stay on the mainland Italy was brief, their sphere of influence on the territorial waters spanned a considerable stretch of time. The Spanish rulers of Sicily assumed a negative stance towards Turkish forces in the Mediterranean on the grounds that they were enemies of Christianity and were also in league with an imperial rival, France. For instance, King John II, who shared the sentiments of his predecessors, prohibited the islanders from engaging in any commercial activities with the Turks. However, the prohibition backfired as the merchants and the Sicilian parliament petitioned the king to revise and revoke his decision. With the help of intimidation, and lobbying, the king held on to the ban and had to remove the viceroy who sided with the local parliament on the Turkish issue. Despite taking its toll on the Sicilian markets, the ban was circumnavigated thanks to clandestine relations the merchants held with Turkish pirates. Lucrative as it was, piracy was also a major problem for the coastal cities of Sicily, for, by the seventeenth century defenses were continued to be built to protect the civilians from being captured and sold into slavery. Turkish pirates were not only threatening the freedom of the ordinary civilians but also of the nobility, and in one particular instance they re-kindled old feuds and enmities between the two most powerful families of the island and thus were an indirect cause of a bloody civil strife.[10]

The Sicilian folktale "The Sultan with the Itch," is a story that runs parallel to the history of the island and incorporates the historical accounts on the latifundia economy and on the relations with the Turks that generally revolved around piracy and unauthorized trade activities. In this respect, the tale could be taken as a cultural product of its milieu, reflecting but also co-opting the socioeconomic conditions of the society of which it is a part.

The tale's hero Pidduzzu is a young man of humble origins who lives with his fisherman father. One day, the boy catches a big fish and decides to offer it to the king as a present. The king, pleased with the act, awards the boy with fifty crowns and asks him if he wants to stay at the royal palace. Joyfully, the little fisherman accepts the proposal and he attains the title Don after a long education in decorum and palace politics. As he grows into an attractive, young man, it turns out that the king's beautiful daughter Pippina falls in love with him. Yet, unfortunately, a son of another king asks for the hand of the princess and as Don Pidduzzu's bloodline has no royal drop in it, the king sanctions the marriage. Pippina confronts her father and makes it clear that she will not give her hand to anyone unless it is Don Pidduzzu. As a consequence of her bold resistance, the

---

10 The spark that ignited the bloody conflict began with the capture of a member of nobility by the Turkish pirates. The pirates asked for a ransom fee for the release of the hostage and the two most powerful families of the city of Sciacca, Lunas and Perollos, stepped up to pay the demanded amount. Eventually, the Turks accepted the Perollos' offer, unleashing a vendetta that would continue for centuries and leave its scars on the city. Please see Giuseppe Quatriglio's *A Thousand Years in Sicily: From the Arabs to the Bourbons* (2005) for further reading.

king sends her away to a convent and discharges Pidduzzu from his service. The princess finds a book of magic in her cell, left there by a "nun-turned-sorcerer" and hands the book to her lover Pidduzzu who happens to stay at an inn in close quarters to the convent. The next day, the king visits his daughter and the princess comes up with a proposal that would settle down the matter once and for all. She convinces the father to give Pidduzzu a brigantine and let the two prospective grooms sail the seas in search of the best and the most precious treasures. Whoever comes with the worthy cargo, she adds, should be the winner of her hand. Delighted, the king accepts the solution and the two suitors immediately take to the sea.

On his way, Pidduzzu opens the magic book and comes across an instruction which reads: "Tomorrow, dock at the first land you come to; go ashore with the whole crew and a crowbar" (Calvino 557). He does as the book commands, and opens the trapdoors with the crowbar until he reaches stairs that descend into a room full of gold. After carrying the precious metals to the ship, he sets sail again and a second instruction appears in the book, which, this time, tells him to disembark on an island, descend into a cave full of food and take the jar on the left without eating anything. It turns out that this jar contains a balm that is able to cure every sickness in the world. Thinking it is high time to go home, Pidduzzu steers his ship to the port of Palermo, alas, he is intercepted and taken prisoner by Turkish pirates. Pidduzzu and his captain are brought to the presence of the sultan, and the sultan, upon learning that the men are from Sicily, orders his men to feed the Sicilians with bread and water only and put them to work in the quarries. One day, Pidduzzu eavesdrops on the conversation Turkish guards have about the incurable itch that ails the sultan. Offering to cure the sultan's ailment in exchange for his freedom and for the valuable cargo on board of his ship, Pidduzzu appears before the sultan for a second time. The sultan accedes to his demands right away but Pidduzzu sets conditions. He asks for a written permission to embark his ship to ensure that his treasures were not stolen by the pirates. The permission is issued and to his relief the cargo is untouched since "these were pirates of honor." Eventually, Pidduzzu helps the sultan to get well and sails off to Palermo. He beats the other suitor with the enormous treasures he brings and marries the princess of Sicily. His parents, "still going barefoot," are invited to the palace and are provided for "in a manner befitting a prince's mother and father" (Calvino 559).

For Claude Levi-Strauss, folktales are a lightly vitiated forms of myths, and just like the mythological stories, folktales can and should be interpreted along diachronic and synchronic axes of analysis. The former axle enables a researcher for a diachronic line of interpretation; "a historical account of the past," and the latter, synchronic dimension would procure the "instrument of interpretation of the present or future" (Meletinsky 26). In his studies on folk lores and myths, Strauss prefers to give equal credence to both approaches since he develops a framework of analysis that is based on "two-dimensional time referent which is simultaneously diachronic and scynchronic" (Lévi-Strauss 212). Such "two-dimensional" model of interpretation is essential to comprehend the principle of opposition and the nature of co-existing contradictions in any folk narrative. Levi-Strauss uses this model to read the myth of Oedipus and comes to the conclusion that the myth is an uneasy resolution of the two opposing worldviews at the time: "the inability. . .to find satisfactory transition between" the cultural belief that mankind has authchtonous origins and the knowledge that "human beings are actually born from the union of man and woman" (216). The story of Oedipus replaces this original schism with yet another contradiction: "born from different or born from same?"

As a matter of fact, Lévi-Strauss considers the existence of oppositions as a quintessential characteristic of a folk narrative for he believes that "mythical thought always works from the awareness of oppositions towards their progressive mediation" (224), the reason why, he further explains, the intermediary figures-terms such as coyote, raven, mist, and scalp are frequently used not to resolve the looming tensions but to defer them. In the preceding pages, it is argued that Turkish characters in Italian folktales, specifically in the tales that are covered in this study, fulfill certain roles. They are treated as figures of ridicule as in "Science of Laziness" tale only to disguise the real addressee of the contempt directed by the subaltern groups. Or they are given a secondary and yet more positive role, as was discussed in "Fair Brow," to complement the moral quest the hero undertakes in his attempt to rehabilitate the deteriorating relations between the landed gentry and the landless peasants.

In a similar vein, "The Sultan with the Itch" makes use of Turkish characters with an aim to postpone the raging conflicts and contradictions that afflicted the Sicilian society in the fifteenth and the sixteenth centuries. The latifundia economy, based on the cultivation of staple crops on huge tracks of land owned by feudal lords, left the majority of the people without land to till and they had to hurdle hunger threshold. Beyond any doubt, Pidduzzu and his family were one of those families who had to scrape a living by going to the sea; either by fishing or by illicit trades with bandits on the Mediterranean. Following Strauss's "awareness of oppositions," we can identify the first binary opposition in the tale. The land stands for ownable, immovable properties, which are unfortunately in the hands of a select few, while the Mediterranean represents mobility and goods that can quickly change hands. Morever, the land is a strictly regulated, and surveilled space on which the power of a central authority, of a king, reigns somewhat supreme whereas the sea is less controlled and monitored zone and thus offers greater liberty for the underprivileged strata of the Sicilian society.

The Turkish characters stand at the junction of this land/sea dichotomy and could be said to prevent one predicate, say the land, the monarchy, from devouring the other by providing a relief valve for the pent up pressure caused by class interests and frictions. The Turkish characters also enable a porous border between the two oppositions and make it possible for a member of one opposition to gain admittance by the other as one of its own. Pidduzzu's story encapsulates the situation well, as his admission into the chambers of affluence and authority conveys a message to the poor populations that it is indeed possible to climb the social ladder if one proves his worth. Pidduzzu's worth is tested and affirmed by his expeditions that take him to the ports of Istanbul and back to Palermo. In other words, his shift from one social standing to that of a 'superior' one is mediated by an exoteric ethnicity that poses a threat for the existence of both the land and the sea. The Ottomans are the enemies of Sicily's inhabitants and rulers, yet, interestingly enough, they are employed as useful antagonists in the story and such sympathetic positioning may be imputed to the historical accounts in which the Sicilians wanted to be given the right to trade freely with the Turks. Pidduzzu's cursory yet candid remark "these were pirates of honor" might nicely dovetail with the history of the island, and, he further consolidates his and the islanders' sociable feelings towards the Turks by helping their leader to get rid of the terrible irritation.

The amicable relations between the Sicilians and the Ottomans may be traced to a practical reason such as free trade, but it is also possible to attribute those relations to another historical layer of the island and to another binary opposition. The Arab rule in Sicily left enduring traces on the culture of the island influencing various wakes of life including administration, architecture, agriculture, fishery, culinary arts and language. As for the ethnic composition of the island, Sicily could be counted as one of the most diverse locations in Italy with its genealogical lines dating back to the first millennium B.C. and extending as far as Tunisia, Anatolia, Syria, and Greece (Rickards, Labarga, Scano, et al. n.p.). Betwixt between Eastern and Western socio-cultural modalities, the island was and has been a meeting point for different ethnicities and cultures and it is possible to encounter such cultural liminality reflected in Sicilian folk culture. The Ottoman Empire in the fifteenth and the sixteenth centuries ruled over much of the lands the Sicilians traced their ancestry to, and the imperial subjects from Greece, the Middle East and the North Africa, if it is not too far-fetched a claim to make, were distant cousins of the islanders. Some sources claim that Don

Pidduzzu's tale is a metamorphosed version of a Greek story of Democedes of Crotone who, just like Pidduzzu, is captured by the Persians and thanks to his abilities in medicine, he heals the king Darius's sprained ankle and cures the breast tumor of the queen Atossa. He finally returns home to Crotone, Italy and marries the daughter of a local magnate.

If one is to match the characters in both tales, the Ottomans as the counterparts of the Persians and Pidduzzu as the Sicilian version of Democedes would be too evident parallelisms to miss. Less obvious analogies can be drawn between Darius and the Turkish Sultan and between Pippina and Atossa. By curing the injured foot of the Persian king, Democedes unintentionally paves the way for the invasion of Greece for he restores mobility to the disabled enemy and plants the idea of invasion in the head of the king by arranging a mock reconnaissance mission that would finally return him home. Pidduzzu, on the other hand, helps the Turkish sultan shed his old skin, recuperate and change the sultan's negative views towards Sicilians, and implicitly, towards Italians. In a roundabout way, Pidduzzu prevents a war between Ottomans and Italian city-states, between Islam and Christianity. An imminent Turkish invasion of the peninsula after the conquest of Constantinople and of Otranto was too substantial a threat the city-states, especially Rome could not ignore. Since the cities were rival of one another, a military campaign launched in the name of Christianity against an infidel army would be the only cohesive reason to rally the troops. In such political conjuncture, Sicily was especially crucial for it was "dangerously poised on the frontier with Islam," and had to be defended at all costs to ensure that "the central and the western Mediterranean would not become an Ottoman lake" (Abulafia 224). Pidduzzu, by crossing into the perilous, unfamiliar zone of Islam and by a safe return to the familiarity of Christianity and his homeland, introduces a transitional segment between two discontinuous schisms. In this respect, Pidduzzu occupies the liminal sites of conflict/non-conflict, of change/non-change, and finally of sovereignty/submission.

In 2013, 12th of May, Pope Francis finalized the long overdue canonization of 813 martyrs of Otranto who were executed by Ottomans in 1480 for their refusal to convert to Islam. Antonio Primaldo and his 812 nameless companions were proclaimed saints by the pope who did not mention Islam in his homily to the congregation gathered in St. Peter's square. Il Giornale, however, a right-wing newspaper owned by Silvio Berlusconi's brother, made it glaringly clear in its headline of the day that 813 were victims of Islam, thus rendering the latent tension and antagonism between Christianity and Islam, between West and East manifest.

Such mixed reactions to the martyrs of Otranto are not unique to Pope Francis's sermon nor to Il Giornale's caption. Francesco Tateo contends that the authenticity of the story of the martyrs has been recently reassessed on the grounds that "the earliest contemporary sources do not support the story of the eight hundred martyrs," and "tales of religious persecution and conscious self-sacrifice for the Christian faith appeared only two or more decades following the siege" (173–174). Between eight hundred and one thousand citizens or soldiers were murdered or captured and sold into slavery after the fall of the city. Still, no official account, Ottoman or Italian, mentions Antonio Primaldo and his 812 companions and their brave stance against professing Islam. Otranto's capture in 1480 and the city's liberation a year after brought to surface a festering political climate that was already ripe in feuds and court intrigues. Following the invasion of the city, Pope Sixtus IV called for an assembly and exhorted all the Christian rulers of Italy to wage a holy war against the invading Ottomans. After retrieving the city, the call for the crusade was immediately forgotten and a rivalry between the newly elected Pope Innocent VIII and the King Ferdinand of Naples picked up steam (İnalcık, 26–31). With the backing up of Venice and Genoa, Pope demanded Ferdinand to pay the vassalage levies and instigated a rebellion by supporting the Anjouan family in Naples. Italy, shortly before the Ottomans' invasion and their subsequent expulsion, found itself at the cross-roads of volatile political matters, in Francesco Guicciardini's words, the country stood upon a delicate balance of powers, and each power center had to act as a check on others' hegemonic consolidation (n.p.). Alliances were quickly forged and easily dissolved, class positions changed almost overnight, men of piety acted as conquerors of cities, merchants invested in art and supported artists. Democracy, feudalism, nipotism, plutocracy, oligarchy, monarchy, and tyranny could co-exist and not cancel each other out.

Political instability brought with it a moral decay that was addressed time and again by a few humanist scholars. Among those scholars Laura Cereta of Brescia (1469–99) is worth giving a special consideration as she didn't refrain from directing her vehement criticism to both male and female humanists who advocated for a militarist solution to the Turkish invasion rather than reformist measures rectifying the social problems. Cereta, calling for an end to futile desires and vain pageantry, inveighed against the depravations in Italy: "We alone, turned away from God, continue to strive; we alone have become lawless and have shaken off every yoke of humanity from our savage minds. Our pardon, however, comes from heaven. Let us be aware, and let us correct the errors of our ways" (139–40). Cereta's rant was not a discrete let alone an idiosyncratic critique of the vices Italy was mired in for it was part of the *modi di pensare* (modes of thinking) that characterized the conceptual shifts in spiritual and material matters at the time. The challenges presented to the divine authority vested in the person of the Pope and to the Catholic Church as the religious leader of the Christian world engendered a "structure of feeling," to borrow Raymond Williams's phrase, that transferred the administrative power, at least in soteriological issues, from clergies to congregations. Benedetto Fontana attributes a major role to humanist scholars for such transition who made it possible to translate ecclesiastical texts "from a language that was the exclusive possession of the ruling castes into one that was the natural vernacular of the people" (37).

"The Slave Mother" tale of Otranto offers a repository of such transformations and paradigm shifts and recounts a story of a mother whose capture by Turkish pirates and bondage in the Ottoman lands bring about a fortunate turn of events both for her forlorn family and for herself. The mother is a devout figure who recites the holy rosary and exerts herself for the happiness of her five sons and husband. On evenings, before sunset and return of the family from the field, the mother sits on the doorway, says her rosary prayers, makes a sign of the cross and then retires home. One day, an owl appears and accosts her with a portentous question whether she desires to be rich in young or old age. Taken aback and frightened by the ominous nature of the question, she refuses to answer the first time. Following her husband's counsel however, she responds to the repeated inquiry and chooses to be rich in old age. After a spell of time, the mother goes out to forage herbs and plants to make a salad of mixed greens. As she bends over to pick up a chicory root, Turkish pirates sneak up on her and carry her away.

The sons and the father mourn for a while, yet "since everything in this world passes," they resume their daily chores. One day, while ploughing a large field, they unearth an iron ring, chained to a stone slab. Providentially, the slab happens to descend to a room containing six mugs brimming with gold, and the jovial company immediately snatches on their good fortune. The gold buys clothes, jewelleries, a big mansion, books, and a berth in *alta società*. The husband and the sons welcome and quickly adapt to such changes and even consider purchasing a slave that would shoulder the burden of menial tasks. It so happens that the slave they would bid for on the auction block turns out to be the hapless mother. Unrecognizable to her husband and sons, and mistaking them for a blue blood family, the mother can't help sighing and silently mourning for her lost family. One evening, the father of the five sons questions her on the reason of her grief and the mother recounts the whole story. The husband recognizes his wife, embraces her and the sons follow suit, comforting her with the following words: "Mamma, you've worked and suffered quite enough. From now on you

will command and enjoy every luxury" (Calvino 455). The tale ends and the re-
united family lives "in the lap of luxury" ever after.

During much of the sixteenth century, the Italian coastal villages, towns, and
cities were far from being safe ports and as a baptismal *fede* from 1693 put it,
much of the Mediterranean and all of the Adriatic coast was a zone "continu-
ally infested by Turks" (Davis, 139). The corsairs from the Barbary coast made
constant forays and they carried away virtually everything that came their way,
yet Italian people, rich or poor, were their main quarry. Held captive for long
periods of time, the prisoners were ransomed for large sums of money. Those
who could afford it could sail back home, yet, those who could not were sold on
auction blocks set in Constantinople, Alexandria, Cairo, Tripoli, Malta, Naples,
and Livorno. On both Christian and Muslim sides, piracy and enslavement were
used as state backed political instruments to weaken the opposition's resources
in man power and capital. Fernand Braudel regards slavery to be a "structural
feature of Mediterranean society" and the Ottomans inherited and incorporated
this structure into their political culture after establishing dominion over the
Mediterranean littoral (*The Mediterranean* n.p.). In fact, the Ottomans and the
corsairs raiding under the banner of the empire were not the sole slave traders
in Mediterranean. Some Christian nations also took part in the lucrative market
and Genoese and Venetian merchants shifted their fields of operation from the
Black Sea and Mediterranean to Atlantic after the closure of the Bosporus by the
Ottoman navy.

In certain respects, "The Slave Mother" tale offers historically tenable narrative strands. Initially, the tale captures well the plight of the subaltern groups who
were the unsuspecting and yet always anxious victims to sudden corsair raids.
The tale also reflects the general feeling of the populations towards enslavement
as some captives celebrated their bondage and welcomed it as a divine test and
opportunity for redemption. In 1678, an Italian slave construed with his slavery
in the following words: "For my sins I was captured in a place called Ascea."
A bleaker account came from a slave in 1735, "I seem to be in another world,
of sufferings and of the torments of Hell" (Davis 176). If the captives remained
true to their Christian faith and weathered the crisis they were facing, a divine
gift would be bestowed on either in their lifetimes or in the hereafter. However,
if their religious mettle succumbed to temptations and if they renounced the
Christian faith and embraced Islam instead, they would be regarded as renegade
confederates of Satan who sold their souls and made pact with an evil denomination. Apparently, the slave mother's captivity lines up with the former category as the mother appears to be a devout Christian in the opening pages of the
tale, yet, the latter issue of conniving with the Devil in return for a gift can also

be accounted for. When the mother returns the owl's question, thanks to her husband's inducement, with a desire to be rich in old age, she pledges her being to an infernal future. The pledge, as it turns out, brings about a wealth as well as a trail of tears for the family.

As mentioned in the opening line of the preceding paragraph, "The Slave Mother" tale includes interestingly accurate historicities that at times move even beyond the pale of mainstream historiographies. The widely accepted view that piracy and slavery in the Mediterranean were solely conducted by eastern factions, mostly by Muslim or Turkish groups that were operating under the banner of the Ottoman Empire is one of those claims invalidated by the tale. The fact that the father and the sons want to buy a slave girl from a slave market set up in the city confirms the presence of a slave economy already in place. As far back as the late 1360s, Venetians were active in slave trade and Francesco Petrarch, in a letter to the archbishop of Genoa, witnessing the unloading of a cargo from one of the Venetian galleys had the following remarks to make albeit with racist undertones.

> Whereas huge shipments of grain used to arrive by ship annually in this city, now they arrive laden with slaves, sold by their wretched families to alleviate their hunger. An unusually large and countless crowd of slaves of both sexes has afflicted this city with deformed Scythian faces, just like when a muddy current destroys the brilliance of a clear one. (956)

Petrarch's blanket use of "Scythian" to describe the slave cargo of the Venetian merchants may be traced to his education and interest in classical literature, but the Venetians would use various terms, in relation to slaves' religious and ethnic origins, and label them as "Tartar, Abkhazi, Circassian, Bulgarian, Russian, Turkish, Greek, Mingrelli" (McKee 306).

The final tale of this chapter featuring Turkish characters is from Giambattista Basile's *Il Pentamerone*, a seventeenth century collection of fairy tales from Basilicata and Campania regions in Southern Italy. The tale is different than the other tales studied in this chapter in respect to its choice of main characters as they are of royal or of noble stock and in relation to its setting for the tale takes place in urban spaces, Constantinople and Napoli, and palaces.

The tale "Rosella" opens with Il Gran Turco's affliction who suffers from leprosy. His physicians, well aware that there is no cure for the Sultan's disease, seek to prolong their doom since a failure to cure his excellency means losing their heads. They make up a story that if the Sultan bathes in the blood of a young prince, his pains would soon be over. The Sultan sends a fleet in search of this young nobility, and the Turkish corsairs happen to find him in "a small boat, sailing slowly on" the seas of Fonte-Chiaro. Back in Constantinople with their valuable cargo, the Sultan's men put prince Paoluccio in chains and leave him in the desolation of the dungeon awaiting his fate. The physicians not happy at all with the capturing of the prince, delay their ruin by another ruse. They say that the prince's blood is livid with anger, and therefore is of no use, so the Sultan should pacify his anger and let the prince's blood calm down. Cajoled, the Sultan places Paoluccio in a beautiful garden where it is always spring, and sends the beautiful Turkish princess to keep him company. As can be guessed easily, the Italian prince and the Turkish princess immediately fall in love. Rosella, the Sultan's daughter, is aware of her father's intentions and trained in geomancy by her queen mother, gives the lover Paoluccio a sword, saying: "O my beauteous muzzle, an thou desire to be free, and to save thy life which is so dear to thee, lose no time; run like an hare to the seaside, where thou shalt find a boat, enter therein and wait my coming, for by the virtue of this charmed sword thou shalt be received by the sailors like an emperor" (Basile 319).

Thanks to the sword, the young prince is welcomed by the sailors "like an emperor" and he is able to find a boat to sail back home. Meanwhile, Rosella casts another magic spell and slips a note in her mother's pocket so that her sleep becomes deep to the point of not hearing the sound of a footstep or of a skirt brushing against the marble floor. Rosella gathers all the valuable jewelries she can get her hands on, and rushes to meet her lover on the harbor. Not long after the lovers set sail, the Sultan and his Queen get the picture of what has transpired, and send a search team after the couple including the Queen mother in company. As the search team bears in on the lovers and the grapple-hooks are thrown, the prince, with his sword, cuts and slashes in every directions and luckily, a swing of the blade cuts off the hands of the Queen and only then the quest to retrieve the lovers is abandoned. In pain, the Turkish Queen curses his daughter that Paoluccio should have no memory of Rosella the moment he steps on his native soil. The Queen Mother relays everything to her husband before giving up her soul, and the Sultan partly due to his loss of his beloved wife and to his disease follows her to afterlife. The curse, however, holds and Paoluccio, soon as he treads the sands of Italy, forgets everything about Rosella. Biting her lips in anguish and remembering her mother's curse, Rosella bides her time for an opportunity to have the prince back.

Glad to see his son back home, the king of Naples organizes an exuberant feast for the young prince, while Rosella, putting her plan into action, rents a palace opposite the residence of the king. Just like insects and bees savoring the sweet smell of an exquisite flower, the young noblemen of Italy buzz around the legendary beauty of the Turkish Princess. Well aware of their carnal desires, Rosella cheats them out of their money by a promise of a sexual consummation. The first cavalier, asked for a thousand ducats to meet the princess, goes to borrow the money from a Jew with a high interest. As the darkness neighs in, Rosella asks the young man to close the door before coming to bed, however, as it is an enchanted door, soon as he closes it, the door opens and this goes on till the first rays of the sun. Dejected, the young nobility withdraws from Rosella's presence. The second night, another member of the genteel class, gains admittance to Rosella's chamber by borrowing a thousand ducats from the merchant. The baron is asked to put out the candle, but the more he blows, the more the candle burns, so he spends all night vainly trying to extinguish the stubborn flame.

The third baron shares the same fate and he wastes his time by combing the hair of the princess "in knotting, and unknotting and trying to put things right" (Basile 323). The three young men eventually disclose to one another the trick played on them and decide to take their case to the king. After listening to their plight, the king sends for Rosella to stand before him, questions and threatens her with the following words "Where didst thou learn to cheat and make fools of my courtiers? Dost thou not think that I will have thee written in the excise book, vile woman, strumpet, lewd piece?" (324). The princess, without disclosing the name of the betrayer, stands her ground and answers the king that she is a "lady of high descent, and the daughter of kings." Upon hearing her words, the king immediately accepts her into his entourage and entreats her to reveal the betrayer. Rosella, taking off a ring from her finger, replies that "The one whose finger this ring fitteth is the unfaithful traitor who hath done me this deed" (325) and throws the ring in the direction of the young prince. The instant the ring lands on Paoluccio's head, he retrieves his memories and rushes to embrace Rosella. After baptizing Rosella in the Christian faith, the Turkish princess and the Italian prince get married.

The "Rosella" tale encapsulates the manifold views the Italian gentry and peasantry held towards the Ottoman/Turkish/Muslim Other accounted for throughout this chapter. The theme of piracy, present in all the tales except for the "Science of Laziness," occupies a central theme in the tale and once again confirms the fears of the Italian people that regardless of one's social status, the threat of enslavement by the Turkish corsairs looms large. Just like piracy and enslavement, the subsequent themes of salvation and repatriation, repatriation with a great amount of wealth, are other common features of the tales that record positive approach to Turkish Other (as is the case with "The Sultan with the Itch," and neutral or covertly negative views as recounted in "The Slave Mother," "Science of Laziness." "Rosella" is no exception to this tradition and provides us with an overt negativity concerning the Turk. In the initial pages of the tale, the

Turkish Sultan and his men, physicians and soldiers, strike us as merciless, cruel characters for they are willing to sacrifice an innocent human being to save his Excellency. We see no heart of change during the captivity of the young prince and the Turkish characters retain, at least halfway to the narrative, their diabolical intentions. Not explicitly stated, their devilish constitutions are somehow related to their religious beliefs, a belief associated with dark magic and pagan ritualistics, and not surprisingly so for the denomination of Islam was commensurate with the concept of Satan for many centuries throughout the continent of Europe. The father Sultan, believing that a bloodbath in a Christian soul would do him good, the Sultana mother, trained in black art, are the two characters that epitomize the "unholy" inclinations of the Muslim world.

The princess Rosella, an expert in sorcery due to her mother's upbringing, chooses to do good with the magical powers at her service. Truly, she employs her powers to cheat the three noble members of the Italian high society, yet she resorts to dark magic only to keep her "chastity" unblemished. The king of Southern Italy, however, threatens Rosella with brandishing her with being a "vile woman, strumpet, lewd piece." In return, the princess keeps her mien and retorts that she is "a lady of high descent and the daughter of kings" and has acted thus only to amend a wrong inflicted on her. The king, after the disclosure of the whole event, gives his assent to the marriage of Rosella and Paoluccio on the condition that Rosella is baptized in the Christian faith. The verses that bring the tale to a conclusion "la nespola, se è còlta acerba e dura, col tempo e con la paglia si matura" ("Ever with time and straw, Thou mayst see the medlar ripen," Basile 325) also imply a termination of the Princess Rosella's acculturation process from an "untamed" nature to a "cultivated" character, from a "heathenish" Ottoman past to a "civilized" Italian future.

III. Moors in Italian Folktales

The Mausoleum of Doge Giovanni Pesaro

Giovanni Pesaro, the doge of Venice from 1658 to 1659, was not a salient member of the *Consilium Sapientium* (the Grand Council) yet, his brief stint in office was granted on account of an impassioned speech he delivered about continuing the war in Crete against the Ottoman forces. Eventually, the Venetian Republic lost the war and the island and Pesaro was in office for a scant one year. Despite a non-remarkable life time, the monument dedicated to Pesaro that can be visited today in the Basilica of Santa Maria Gloriosa dei Frari, in Venice, is a notable sight. The monument consists of a lower and an upper gallery and the ornate design of the mausoleum is tailored to convey a story about Giovanni Pesaro and Pesaro family. The base of the structure rises on the shoulders of four gigantic Moorish figures who carry sacks of a staple crop and the burden of the doge's throne. The throne is held by two dragon-like monsters and the doge addresses the imaginary crowd gathered before his royal chair. Pesaro's tomb re-invokes a well-known pattern in Venetian symbolism: the blackamoor as a servant of the Republic of Venice. During the Renaissance period, servility came to be associated with skin color and "...society at large equated black skin color (of whatever hue) with slavery," and the practice was so commonplace and inured that "many freed ex-slaves were apprehended as fugitives and were forced to negotiate their freedom all over again through the courts" (Lowe 20). In time, however, the word "black" was dissociated from the word "moor" and the latter's etymological definition incorporated both ethnicity and religion, thus making it a vague and a difficult concept to pinpoint. Ethnically, the word "Moro" was used to identify people from [della] "Mauritania, dell'Etiopia, dell'Africa" and religiously those who were thought to be "Saraceno, Musulmano." Despite the attempts to mold it in a familiar shape, the term "Mauros" (Greek), "Moro" (Italian), "Moor" (English) eluded simple definitions: "No wonder, since it ['mauros,' 'Moro'] referred to 'phantoms' difficult to recognize, and in general to the vague concept of darkness" (Bassi 159). In the late 1400s, the floating signifier "Moor" was attached to and fixed by another figure of an Oriental Other. In some Venetian paintings, the conjunction of "Moor" with "Turks" could be seen in the late 1400s and the coinage of the word *turco moro* coincided with the Ottomans' rise in power and the ensuing clashes of interests with the Venetian Republic. Giovanni Pesari's tomb, which surprised some American visitors that there was a "monument to Negro slavery" in Venice, was a testament to such crossing point whereby the

word Moor was commensurate with Ottomans and vice versa (Kaplan 57). For
some historians, the monument with its four colossal Nubian figures was representative of the ethnic diversity under the administration of the Ottoman Empire
at the time, yet, for Paul Kaplan, the four gigantic figures were "more like a set
of captive demons" who evidenced not only "the absolute otherness but also the
absolute baseness of Venice's enemies" (ibid.). Nevertheless, the monument was
meant as an indemnification for the loss of Crete to the Ottomans and for its
"crass assertion of a racially based hegemony. . ..meant to compensate for an
increasing loss of actual power" (ibid.).

Despite the efforts at conjoining African, Turkish and Muslim identities in
the official lexicon, the creation and the crystallization of a single entity, of an
ultimate Otherness fell through for no unified, solidifying discourse was available to the Republic of Venice and to the Italian city states at the time. Even
amongst the Venetians there was dissent and mixed feelings as to the meaning
of the Ottomans for the Republic's welfare. Fernand Braudel claims that even
after the fall of Constantinople in 1453, the Republic was quick to realize that
a peaceful coexistence with the Ottomans was vital in maintaining the valuable trade posts and routes. By April 1454, the Signoria signed a peace treaty
with the Emperor of the Turks since it was next to impossible for Venice to "live
without the Turks, without their cheap raw materials and the huge markets they
represented" (Braudel *Out of Italy* 284). Besides the lucrative trade deals, the
Venetians' relations with the Ottomans were so dangerously intimate at times
that "several Venetian noblemen of ancient family- a Grimani, a Tron, an Emo"
could go so far as to state that there was "no redemption for our affairs than lea-
guing ourselves with Turks and bringing them into Italy" (Niccoli 57).

Although no encompassing and all-convincing storyline was in place to con-
junct African, Ottoman and Muslim identities, a few attempts were made to that
end. Portents, prophecies, visions, divinations that were customarily pinned on
fanciful imagination of folk culture were systematically manipulated and re-
worked as instruments of propaganda. In different parts of Italy, visions of a war
between two great armies were reported and one vision in particular in Bergamo
countryside caught the attention of the ecclesiastic authorities. In the original
version, oxen, sheep and pigs were reported in the aftermath of the great battle,
however, once the oral account was turned into a Roman pamphlet, its peasant
roots were removed "by placing the pigs in an ecclesiastical tradition that, as
early as twelfth century, saw pigs as an incarnation of sin and vice" (Niccoli
84). In another written copy of the vision, the pigs personifying "sin and vice"
were judged by the populace to signify "the Mahometan infidels" (Niccoli 83).
In an effort to create anti-Turkish sentiment and to generate a consensus for a

crusade against the Ottoman Empire, Pope Leo X was eager to propagate the re-processed versions of the visions. This was one of the many attempts to correlate the religion of Islam with the Turkish ethnicity and with the color "black" that alluded to "physiognomies (dark skin, full lips, broad noses, tightly curled hair) to characterize some Ottoman subjects" (Kaplan 41).

As was noted earlier, the sixteenth century Italy was a medley of numerous political formations and there was no consensus among the city states concerning their relations with the Ottoman Empire. Despite being the main purveyor of opinions and of information about the Ottomans, *La Serenissima* was not the sole Italian agent in the Near East. Enjoying a semi-autonomous status under the Byzantines and the Ottomans, the Genoese community in Istanbul continued to flourish until their lapse from grace as the "most favored nation" in the seventeenth century (Mitler 79). The Florentines, trying to maintain their share of the trading profits, sought to depose the Venetians from their seat of power in the Near East and attempted to disrupt the relations between Venice and the Ottomans (Rossi 8). In their turn, the Venetians, against a nascent yet capable rival, interfered in Rimini-Istanbul relations and arrested the engraving artist Matteo de' Pasti on his way to Istanbul on the alleged charges of espionage. An alliance with the Ottomans, aside from the economic yields, was vital to gain the upper hand in the political tug-of-war between the Italian city-states (Rossi 9–10). In this regard, the pursuit to lump Muslims, Moors and Turks together was a stillborn act and did not find supporters among both the ruling classes and the subaltern groups for Turks, Muslims and Moors were respectively related to different historical periods and cultural thought ways of Italy and were used to refer to un-uniform significations.

On the official level, such ramifications as to the import and imbrication of a race, a creed and an ethnicity as the ultimate Other are well documented and one needs to peruse the works such as Fernand Braudel's *Out of Italy: Two Centuries of World Domination and Demise* and *A History of Civilizations*, Alessandro Barbero's *Barbari: Immigrati, profughi, deportati nell'impero romano* and *Straniero: L'invasore, l'esule, l'altro,* and Marino Formica's *Lo specchio turco: Immagini dell'altro e riflessi del sé nella cultura italiana d'età moderna*. On the reception of foreigners by the "common folk," Ottavia Niccoli's *Prophecy and People in Renaissance Italy* provides some valuable information as to the worldviews of the Italian peasantry in the fifteenth and the sixteenth centuries and the deliberate co-option of those views by certain ruling classes of Italy. It is important to note, however, as it was argued in the preceding chapter, that regarding the figures of the Other(s) there were a few cases in which the approaches of both the higher and the lower echelons of the Italian society followed a parallel and at times converging trajectories. Culling its primary sources from Italian folktales once again, and taking its cue from the claim that folktales present thetic and antithetic discourses to a hegemony, this chapter puts forward two main propositions regarding the equivocal positions of Moorish characters in Italian folk literature. First, it is argued that Moors in Italian folklore occupy a different plane of meaning than that of Turkish characters since their presence in the Italian peninsula can be followed back as far as the eighth century CE and they lived on the tip of the peninsula and on Sicily for a considerable time either as domestic servants, merchants or local landlords (Gabrieli and Scerrato). Turks, on the other hand, except for a brief occupation of Otranto in 1480, did not remain long on the peninsula yet their presence in Europe was perceived by the Italian states as a constant threat to their existence and to Christianity. In other words, Moors were proximate and familiar "Others" in Italy whereas Turks were distant and exotic enemies. Secondly, the allusions made to the skin color of Moorish characters in Italian folktales bring to the fore the issue of race and in this respect Moors are studies as part of a complex marginalization process that put them at the crossroads of variegated historical and cultural modalities. Speaking of intricate socio-cultural relations, it would be pertinent to put in a few words about William Shakespeare's famous tragedy *Othello* for the play nicely encapsulates and reiterates the two points given above.

Set in Venice, the story revolves around a Moorish general in the Venetian army and much depends on him to vanquish the Ottoman fleet in the Mediterranean. Virginia Mason Vaughan, in her historicist work *Othello: A Contextual History* aptly captures the intricacies involved when Shakespeare wrote and staged his famous tragedy: "[*Othello*] exploits ... perceptions of a global struggle between the forces of good and evil, a seeming binary opposition that in reality is complex and multifaceted" (Vaughan 27). Othello stands at the junction of this multifaceted reality and embodies the fears and the anxieties of "turning Turk"; "the fear of a black planet that gripped Europeans in the early modern era as they faced the expansion of Ottoman power." (Vitkus 146) In this chapter, the Moorish characters in Italian and Turkish folktales are studied in a similar vein, namely, just like Othello, the Moors in the tales are claimed to occupy ambiguous and complex positions within the imaginary landscapes of the Italian populace and those ambivalent positions are addressed within "communally shared repertoire of conventions, and the institutions and practices" (Greenblatt 12) of Italian society and within the cultural milieus of their productions.

The Penumbra of Death

In the second chapter of this book, Antonio Gramsci's idea of hegemony and Claude Levi-Strauss' structural model are given as conceptual points of departure to study the functions of the Turkish characters in the Italian folk narratives. Posited as intermediary figures, the Turkish characters are claimed to play a mediating role between two or more incommensurable social realities as depicted in the studied folktales. In this chapter, however, a paradigm shift in theoretical framework is introduced due to the unique position of the Moorish characters in Italian folk literature. The Moors in the tales either face death in consequence of their "evil" deeds or they are already dead and yet are able to haunt the stories. In this respect, the issue of Otherness or the processes of marginalization should be problematized further and for that matter the terms "vanishing mediator," first introduced by Fredric Jameson, "supplement" as put forward by Jacques Derrida and "homo sacer" by Giorgio Agamben are consulted.

In his widely acclaimed article on Max Weber's narrative structure, Fredric Jameson presents his idea of "vanishing mediator" and postulates that Protestantism has secured the transition from Medieval ethos to modern capitalism and the religious reform movement has acted in the capacity of "a catalytic agent" enabling "exchange of energies between two otherwise mutually exclusive terms." Once the task of mediation is accomplished, the "overall bracket. . .within which change takes place" could be taken apart and discarded for its usefulness would no longer be needed (Jameson 78). It is hard to miss certain parallelisms between Jameson's "vanishing mediator" and Claude Levi-Strauss' intermediary figures in mythical thought. A *prima facie* affinity could be set regarding their unique positions of balancing two incompatible and even contradictory perceptions of social reality. Jameson sees Protestantism as the equilibrant term and Levi-Strauss posits coyotes and ravens as counterbalancing forces. There is, however, one stark difference that distinguishes their respective stances on mediation. In Levi-Strauss' formula, the tension between two clashing world views are not resolved and a transition from one camp to the other is ensured by mediation. As it is claimed in the previous chapter, the opposing parties defer their imminent tensions via an intermediary figure and leave them for future, possible solutions. Thus, the contradiction regarding the case of the King Oedipus is not solved by providing an answer to the question whether human beings have authchtonous roots or are born from the union of man and woman but further contrasted and deepened by yet another opposition: "born from different or born from same?" (Lévi-Strauss 216). Since the contradiction and the accompanying tension are reproduced by fission, the same argument could be made for the fate of the intermediary figures for they need to be re-invented whenever contradictions loom large over a society.

In Jameson's analysis, if my reading is assumed to be correct, the mediating agent does not vanish prematurely but remains in place until an unproblematic transition is completed. Its dismantling is decided in relation to its usefulness and if no use could be found for the mediator, it vanishes. The ruminations whether the mediator dissipates without a trace or becomes invisible while retaining some of its potency or resurges time and again but suppressed by a counter agent may lead the discussion nowhere, yet an attempt to tackle them could allow for another reading which may shift the perspective. Juxtaposing Fredric Jameson's "vanishing mediator" with Jacques Derrida's "supplement" should support such theoretical shift. The "supplement," thanks in part to Derrida's abstruse style, is a difficult term to pinpoint for it entails a maddening rationale: "it is neither presence nor absence, neither inside nor outside, and/or both inside and outside at the same time. It forms part without being part, it belongs without belonging" (Royle 49). In *Specters of Marx*, Derrida further complicates the supplement's position by calling it a ghostly concept, impossible to "arrest, domesticate and tame" (Derrida *Of Grammatology* 50). The spectrality of supplement, like the ghost of Hamlet's father, opens up the risk of turning everything that is held certain and stable into "uncertain, undone, disjoined" entities (Lucy 112). Thus, it can be surmised that in Derrida's terminology the term "supplement" may act like a de-stabilizer agent that unsettles boundaries and problematizes the distinctions between an inside and an outside (Royle 50) and as Simon Wortham indicates, it is added to or adds itself on an "ideal or original presence" disclosing "the lack and self-difference" in an already divided "origin of presence" (204). Both Jameson and Derrida are notorious for their hard to tackle ideas and it is the least of my concerns to rub salt into the wound. The tale "Le Ossa del Moro" ("The Moor's Bones") from Benevento, Campania, blurring the lines between the living and the dead, between distinct shapes of self and shadowy outlines of Moorish Other, should help us dispel the theoretical haze. As is the wont of the present study to furnish the tales with a historical backdrop, the analysis of "The Moor's Bones" should commence with a historical overview of Benevento and Campania and of the presence of Moors in Southern Italy.

The history of Benevento and of Campania is shrouded in mystery since many historians of Medieval Europe preferred to turn a blind eye or paid little attention to the region. Indeed, the secondary sources that address the Southern Italy's relations with the Islamic world from the seventh to ninth centuries are very scarce (Kreutz 32). In terms of political intrigues and civil strife, however, Campania was no different than other regions in Italy. The towns of Benevento,

Bari, Amalfi and Salerno were the usual battle grounds between Neopolitans and Lombards and to gain the upper hand in the protracted warfare the warring factions hired Muslim mercenaries from the North African Berber tribes. Except for brief intervals of peace, hiring of the Muslim soldiers of fortune continued for centuries and in due course the mercenaries began to settle down in the cities they were paid to fight for. Leasing or selling of farm lands to Muslims by the peasants of Benevento and Salerno were not uncommon transactions and the descriptions such as *terra sarracini* (Saracen land) and *locum spianu maiure*, "the place of the Spanish Moor" were used to indicate the Muslim proprietors of the lands (Kreutz 250-51). The growing numbers of Muslims in Campania worried Pope John VIII to such an extent that he threatened the cities harboring the mercenary bands with excommunication or induced the rulers to "give up 'the society' of the Saracens" and to break their "evil alliances" in return for an annual payment of 10,000 *mancusi*. (Kreutz 278). Pope John's anxieties were not unwarranted as the Muslims from the North Africa, exploiting the instability in the region, found footholds that would later lead to the establishment of the Emirate of Bari. Little is known about the history of the Emirate that lasted from 847 to 871, yet some very interesting events, at times embellished for a poetic effect, took place during that brief period and in the subsequent years following the downfall of the Emirate. The theme of turning, of a native Italian becoming a Saracen was one of the foremost concerns that troubled the local administrators. An Italian could go "to the other side" to avoid punishment or become a Muslim corsair for illicit profits. Despite their rarity, there were even a few cases of interethnic, interfaith marriages that sometimes caused controversies as to the religious education of the children (Berto 126–136). Among such various accounts of interactions, one event stands out with its intriguing plotline that display some parallelisms with the tale of "'The Moor's Bones."

After being captured by the men of the marquise of Tuscany, Bertha, a eunuch named Ali entered the non-military service of the marquise and carried her dispatches to the Caliph al-Mü'ktafi in Baghdad. A long letter, along with a long trail of gifts of "weapons, Slav slaves, huge dogs, falcons, hawks, birds able to detect poisoned food and beads aiding the extraction of spearheads" were entrusted to the care of the eunuch Ali to deliver to the Caliph. The letter, extolling the might of the Caliph, also boasted of the power the Queen possessed. The Queen Bertha held indeed a considerable power in her hands as her sway extended "over twenty-four kingdoms" and "the great city of Rome" was also a part of her great kingdom (al-Rashīd 93). The letter ended with a mysterious message that was to be conveyed to the Caliph by the eunuch and was to be given orally and the contents of the message were to remain secret between the

Queen, Ali and the Caliph. Nothing is known about the substance of the dispatch, yet, from the Caliph's reply to the Queen we at least know that the message found its addressee. The Queen Bertha enjoyed a posthumous fame in the
fifteenth and sixteenth centuries and was even elevated to the status of a saint
due to her angelic actions. According to the legends and the stories attributed
to her name, on Christmas Eves and accompanied by "a host of playful spirits,
elves, nixes, kobolds, and dwarves," the Queen would wander about, see "to justice in households" and punish the disorderly residents (Rumpf 185). She would
wield her power not by a scepter or a royal mace but by a spindle, thus she would
be seen not as a domineering figure with imperial ambitions but as a "humble
woman" with modest aspirations.

On the basis of her letters to the Caliph, quite an opposite character to that
of an unassertive woman could be portrayed. As can be inferred from her letter
to al-Mü'ktafi, Bertha was ambitious in her plans to extend her sphere of influence in Europe and was eager to maintain her grasp on the throne. She might be
and probably was a woman of charity who founded churches and monasteries
and came to the rescue of those in need, nevertheless, she was also a visionary
to seek the alliance of a formidable empire of its time. The tales on Bertha have
had Germanic origins and they were especially popular in Bohemia, Austria,
Germany, and Switzerland. Jacob Grimm traced the provenance of the tales to
a Germanic pre-Christian goddess Frau Holle and felt that there were certain
connections between the goddess and Queen Bertha of Burgundy, the Queen of
the Franks (Rumpf 191). Despite her appeal in Germanic lands, the Queen did
not enjoy a legendary status in Italy and it may even be propounded that she was
not very welcome due to the deep seated aversion to foreign rule in the peninsula. In *Straniero: L'invasore, l'esule, l' altro*, Alessandro Barbero touches upon
this delicate subject of strangers' hegemony in Italy which instilled feelings of
hostility in Italian subjects:

> "il sostegno delle baionette austriache ai duchi di Parma o di Modena, e di quelle francesi
> al papa-Re, fissa per sempre l'associazione fra potere tirannico e potere straniero."
> (Barbero 45)
> ("the support of the Austrian bayonets to the dukes of Parma or Modena, and of the
> French ones to the Pope-King, forever fixed the association between tyrannical power
> and foreign power.")

The tale "Le Ossa del Moro" is a story about a queen who seizes the throne after
the death of the king and whose Moor lover is killed by her stepson. On the
surface, the tale may look like another Italian tale that features conventional
themes and characters underlining various Italian folk stories. Giving it a second

glance, it is possible to discern certain connections between the historical figure of queen Bertha and the fictional persona of the queen in "The Moor's Bones." Bearing a grudge towards the Moor lover of his stepmother, the prince lures him into the thick of the forest on the pretext of going hunting, kills him on the spot and then buries his corpse. The queen, fearing the worst, takes her dog along and sets out in search of her lover. The dog's sensitive nose detects the odor of the crime and digs and digs until the skull and the bones of the poor Moor are exhumed. The queen collects what remains of her lover and orders the skull to be molded into a drinking cup adorned with gold and precious gemstones, the leg bones into a chair and the arms into a frame of a mirror. Unwilling to let her son go unpunished, she summons him to her presence and says: "You killed the Moor, so I'm condemning you to death. I will spare you only if, in three months' time, you can explain the meaning of this riddle: 'I drink Moor, I sit Moor, I look up and see Moor'" (Calvino 421). The son wanders from town to town, village to village in search of the answer to the riddle. A day before the prescribed time expires, the hapless youth comes upon a family living in a haystack in a forlorn territory. Famished, he asks for food but the miserable father and mother reply that they have nothing to offer. The beautiful daughter, however, feeling pity for the young man and sensing him to be of royal stock, slaughters the only hen they possess and feeds him. In the night, the prince wakes up and hears the daughter whisper to her mother.

> "Did you notice how the king's son carved the hen? He gave Papa the legs, since he goes out and gets food for us. He gave you the breast, since you are the mother and nursed me as a baby. He gave me the wings, since 1 am beautiful like an angel of paradise. And he ate the head himself, since he will be his subjects' head." (ibid.)

Realizing the shrewdness of the girl, the prince decides to ask her the riddle. "That's easy," she replies, "'I drink Moor' refers to the queen's drinking cup. 'I sit Moor' refers to her chair. 'I look up and see Moor' refers to her mirror" (ibid.). The prince thanks her, leaves a pouch of gold and promises to return to marry the girl. After his return to his father's kingdom, he pretends not to have an answer to the riddle and while his neck is in the noose, the crowds gathered in the shadow of the gallows begin crying "spare him!" The queen, fearing the wrath of the populace, grants him a second chance to answer the riddle. This time, the young prince presents the solution to the puzzle "and" he adds "the riddle in its entirety means that the queen must hang for thinking of the Moor, both living and dead, and forgetting my late father" (Calvino, 422). The queen is sent to the gallows, the prince marries the wise maiden living in the haystack and sits on the throne bequeathed by his father.

The progression of the tale follows a usual path expected of a folk narrative. The villainous stepmother usurps the throne, is in league with a foreigner, unjustly banishes the true heir and eventually meets her death after justice is served. The hero leaves his home, is helped by a poverty-stricken family, returns home, regains the throne and marries the virtuous and beautiful girl who helps him in his travails. Put next to the historical account of Queen Bertha and her exchanges with the Caliph of Islam, the tale's narrative course takes a different turn. Conjectural though it may sound, disembodied and inarticulate, the ghost of the Moor nevertheless talks beyond his grave. The dead Moor's bones, his haunting remainders cannot be subsumed to the signifying chain of the tale and therefore continue to disturb the spatial ontologies of the tale. His words point beyond the pale of an amorous relationship to imperatives of *ontopology*.[11]

The Moor appears out of blue right at the beginning of the story and there is no detail whatsoever as to the how or why his presence is thus abruptly presented. It may be surmised that he is present even before the death of the king, possibly a high-ranking mercenary in the king's army, and possibly an acquaintance of the prince since he readily agrees to join his hunting party. The late king seems to preserve the integrity of the boundaries, the thresholds of his kingdom despite some "foreign" elements within and yet after his death those borders become porous and susceptible to unsettling changes. The first example of such disturbances is the transference of power from a patriarchal position to a matriarchal one. The queen's succession to the throne instead of the prince deals a blow to the gender roles set in place to regulate the social norms that assign women to the hearths of their homes and men to the main squares of the towns. The insertion of the domestic, of the private domain into the public sphere means overstepping a threshold that presumably safeguards the differences constructed around masculine and feminine identities. In *The Witch in History: Early Modern and Twentieth Century Representations*, Diane Purkiss points out to a conviction that in early modern thought, both in elite and popular imagination, body was believed to be "flowing with humours or liquids, resembling a bag full of potentially polluting substances" (119). Similarly, Elizabeth Grosz writes that the perception of body as a vessel of contamination has remained one of the constants in Western culture and has been associated with femininity:

---

11 By ontopology, Jacques Derrida means "an axiomatics linking indissociably the ontological value of present – being [on] to its situation, to the stable and presentable determination of a locality, the topos of territory, native soil, city, body in general" (Derrida *Specters of Marx* 103) and the term is used in line with the context Derrida provides.

> Can it be that in the West, in our time, the female body has been constructed not only as a lack or absence but with more complexity, as a leaking, uncontrollable, seeping liquid; as formless flow; as viscosity, entrapping, secreting; as lacking not so much or simply the phallus but self-containment—not a cracked or porous vessel, like a leaking ship, but a formlessness that engulfs all form, a disorder that threatens all order? (203)

Taking Purkiss's and Grosz's insights as points of departure, the queen and the lover in "The Moor's Bones" can be said to epitomize such "formlessness" that threatens to "contaminate" and plunge the kingdom into chaos. The frontiers between order and disorder, legal and illegal, sacred and profane, normal and abnormal are transgressed by the queen not once but twice since, after her seizure of power, she chooses a man with a dark complexion, an exotic ethnicity and an inimical religion for her partner in power. Thus, the corporeality of the Moor already hints at a perilous liminal presence and his desolidifed body turned into paraphernalia augments the danger of blurring the boundaries in Benevento society. The prince's quest to solve the riddle, to bring the pieces together into a coherent whole could be said to symbolize the attempt to eliminate the dangers posed by the presence of the queen and the absence of the Moor. The prince's marriage with the poor girl living in the haystack restores a modicum of order as the girl has a humble bearing and, unlike the queen, has a strict sense of hierarchies and of social roles: "He gave Papa the legs, since he goes out and gets food for us. He gave you the breast, since you are the mother and nursed me as a baby. He gave me the wings, since I am beautiful like an angel of paradise. And he ate the head himself, since he will be his subjects' head" (Calvino 421). Jacques Derrida defines the notion of trace not as a presence but rather as "the simulacrum of presence that dislocates, displaces and refers beyond itself" (Derrida "Differance" 295). In certain regards, Derrida's remarks on trace could be interlaced with his exposition of "supplement." Concerning the ipseity of an individual or *raison d'être* of an administration, both the trace and the supplement seem to play similar roles in interrupting the full presence of a system and in suspending established conventions, moralities, norms and laws. The trace and the supplement, in their umbrageous potentials, are likely to cast their shadows over the sureties of existence and thus create an alterity, an otherness that cannot be assimilated into the fabrics of societal formations. The Moor's body, killed, buried and later exhumed to be used as the personal furniture of the queen, constitutes such alterity, a trace and a supplement that imperil the integrity of the kingdom by opening a hole in the homogeneity of the social body. In *Raising the Dead: Readings of Death and (Black) Subjectivity*, Sharon Patricia Holland contends that the "desires" not the "bodies" of the dead are exhumed and utilized by the state, thus "by ensuring control of the corpse, society ensures control of its opposite, the living nation" and "the ability of the emerging nation to speak hinges on its correct use of the 'dead' in the service of its creation" (28). The prince, accompanied by his devoted and virtuous wife seem to be accomplishing this feat of founding a new nation and the Moor's bones look like proper instruments in realizing such achievement. Death may or may not be coterminous with race but it is a significant register to comprehend the experiences of slave populations in Italy and to address the complexities surrounding the Moorish characters in Italian folktales. Hence, the following section opens with a brief historical survey of slavery in Italy.

The Enemy Within

During the fifteenth and the sixteenth centuries, the cargo ships carried slaves from diverse ethnicities into the ports of Venice, Genoa, Palermo, and Naples. According to Salvatore Bono, in the sixteenth century Sicily, black African slaves comprised nearly half of the slave population due to the island's trade relations with the corsairs and its proximity to the slave markets in Africa. The prices set for the slaves with darker complexions were considerably less compared to the lighter skinned ones. Sally McKee attributes the price discrepancy to Italians' "prejudice against dark-skinned people" (312). Amidst such pre-conceived negative dispositions, however, there was a remarkable exception that sometimes verged on an obsessive interest in black bodies. Isabella d'Este, daughter of Ercole I d'Este, Duke of Ferrara and spouse of Francesco Gonzaga, Marquis of Mantua, was fascinated with black child servants and even wrote a letter to her appointee in Venice to obtain a black girl "una moreta" "between the ages of one and a half and four, and twice in early June reminded him of the request, emphasizing that the girl should be 'as black as possible'" (Kaplan 134). On June 14, she wrote a letter to the agent to temporarily halt his search since she was able to lay her hands on an older and yet a fine prospect: "We couldn't be more pleased with our black girl even if she were blacker, because from being at first a little disdainful she has now become pleasing in words and acts and we think she'll make the best buffoon in the world" (ibid.).

The black slaves, besides being sought after servants of a few Italian courts, were also the begetters of noble personages. The mother of Alessandro de' Medici, the first Medici duke of Florence, was a freed African slave living in the village of Collevecchio in the vicinity of Rome. A graffito "Hail Alessandro of Collevecchio" was painted on the wall of the duke's residence in Rome to ridicule his origins, yet, the mocking reference was not made to the prince's "African blood" *per se* but to his peasant, "lowly" status deemed to be unbefitting to rule over a great city such as Florence (Brackett 303). The cases of Isabella d'Este and Alessandro de' Medici were exceptions to the harrowing experiences of the slave populations in Italy. On May 1, 1479, the Genoese officials were summoned to investigate the death of a twenty-five-years old Moorish slave woman by the name of Caterina. The investigators found her body hanging from a light fixture and upon examining her corpse, they detected torture marks and bruises on her back and sexual organs. Although there was enough evidence to charge the slave owners with first-degree murder, the authorities closed the case stating that Caterina committed suicide on the spur of a moment of anguish (Epstein 64). The domestic slaves were not entitled to any legal rights and were considered chattels to be included in the inventories of animals: "He says that he has a female slave and a horse and two donkeys and three fifths of an ox. Let us put them down at seventy florins" (Origo 334). Bereft of their families, native tongues, names, and legal rights, the peoples in bondage were on the lowest rung of the social ladder. They were "socially dead," to borrow from Orlando Patterson, who were "ritually incorporated as the permanent enemy on the inside" (39). Similar to Patterson's claim, Iris Origo, in "The Domestic Enemy: The Eastern Slaves in Tuscany in the Fourteenth and Fifteenth Centuries," wrote that in medieval Italy, specifically in Tuscany and Northern Italy, the slaves were at times thought to be dangerous presences. In one such instance, Margherita Datini sent a letter to her husband complaining of the unruly behaviors of her slaves: "They are *femmine bestiali*, you cannot trust the house to them: they might at any moment rise up against you" (342). Datini's fear was not unfounded since there were records of violence committed by the slaves against their masters. The apprehension of the masters grew to such proportions that on 28th of October, 1410, the Grand Council of Venice passed a decree that allowed the investigation of the slaves and the servants by torture if they were caught "making charms or herbs" or putting them "in the food or on the persons of their master" (Origo 340). Such anxieties, for Origo, led to division of the "slave-owning households. . .into two camps with sullen, resentful, half-savage slaves on one side, and on the other, suspicious, and often extremely nervous masters" (ibid.).

The tale "Erbabianca" ("Wormwood") will be addressed in view of the historical outline sketched above as the plot of the tale is analogous in many respects to the archival accounts of the real events. The "Wormwood" recounts the story of a king and a queen whose off-springs, to the king's great dismay, happen to be girls. Seething with rage, the king gives the queen one last chance to bear him a male heir and threatens to have the baby killed if it turns out to be another female. Unfortunately, the queen gives birth to yet another girl and fearing for her baby's life, she entrusts her to the care of her godmother. The poor woman not knowing what to do and in awe of the king's anger, goes into the country and leaves the baby on a wormwood bush. As luck would have it, in that distant countryside lives a hermit who finds the baby nestled in the wormwood bush and carries her to his cave. The hermit shares the cave with a doe and her fawns and he asks the doe to "nurse her" along with her fawns. As time passes by, the baby grows up to be a maiden of exquisite beauty, her royal identity remaining unknown all along. One day the king, not the king the father but a ruler of a different country, goes out hunting but finds himself in the middle of a terrible storm. He sees a faint light glimmering in the distance and walks wearily towards his only shelter. The hermit, realizing the unexpected guest to be the king himself, calls out to his adopted daughter, "Wormwood! Wormwood! Bring a chair, light the fire, and make His Majesty comfortable!" (Calvino 563). Amused by the name of the girl, the king asks the hermit the reason why he calls her by that name. The hermit tells him the story of the bush and how he found the girl. Attracted by the girl's beauty and her refined manners, the king requests to take her with him to his great palace where she can live in luxury and receive a good education. Happy for the bright future thus opened before his foster child, the hermit readily agrees to let her go. After a while at the palace, the girl's true merit begins to shine. She becomes more beautiful and displays a shrewd mind during her instructions. Upon seeing what the girl has become, the king marries Wormwood and she becomes the queen of the kingdom.

Deeply in love, the king rides away one day to meet a company of princes and knights. Probably after a carousal of drinking, the noble men began to sing praises, each boasting of the rare beauties and loyalties of their wives. The king, sure of himself and of her wife, accepts a bet from one of the knights who claims that he can seduce Wormwood during the king's absence. If the knight was successful within a month, he would receive a fief from the king. In Palermo, the knight takes frequent walks under the window of the queen just to catch a glimpse of her, but to no avail since the windows are always shut. Depressed in spirits, the knight is approached by an old woman begging for alms. The vagabond woman assures the knight that he will have access to the queen if he waits patiently. With a basket of eggs and fruits, the woman knocks on the palace door, requesting to speak to the queen. Deceiving the queen into believing that she is a relative of hers, the old woman gains her trust and the right "to go in and out of the queen's room and do whatever she pleased" (Calvino 565). One night, while the queen is asleep, the woman sneaks into her bedchamber, lifts the cover and discovers a beauty spot on her back. With a pair of scissors, the woman cuts the hairs sprouting from the mole and steals away pleased with herself. She meets with the knight, delivers the hairs, mentions the beauty mole gracing the back of the queen, and gives a detailed account of her facial features and for her services the knight pays the woman a generous sum of money.

Back in the presence of the king, the knight describes the physical attributes of the queen down to the minute detail of the mole on her back and even procures the hairs. Brokenhearted, the king hurries back to the palace and orders horses harnessed to a carriage. In a harsh voice he orders Wormwood to climb up and gallops to a spot in the countryside far from his kingdom. Upon reaching the slopes of Mount Pellegrino, he orders her to get down and gives her a violent blow with his whip that knocks her unconscious and rides back to his palace. A few hours later, a convoy comprising a doctor, his wife and his Moorish slave Ali passes by Wormwood's half-dead body. The doctor, suggesting to postpone their trip to the Sanctuary of St. Rosalie for the fulfillment of their vow taken for the birth of their son, attends to Wormwood's wound and carries her back to their home. During her stay with the family, Wormwood refuses to answer the questions regarding her past and her misfortune and despite her hazy history, she wins the confidence of the doctor and his wife so much so that they trust their daughter to Wormwood's care before they resume their journey to St. Rosalie. While their daughter and Wormwood are asleep, the parents set out early in the morning taking their slave Ali along. After going a short distance, Ali pretends to have forgotten the basket lunch. Now this Ali bears a morbid grudge against Wormwood due to the affection his masters have for the maid. Upon returning home, he cautiously approaches the bed where Wormwood and the child sleep and slits the throat of the poor girl. Finding herself drenched in blood and delirious with panic, Wormwood flees into the countryside until her weary legs bring her to a dilapidated palace. She timidly pushes the door open and discerns a decrepit sofa and weary from the day's toils she immediately falls asleep. Meanwhile in the kingdom of Wormwood's father, the queen reveals the truth about the fate of their last child and the king, feeling self-reproach, departs in search of his daughter and comes upon a partially decayed palace in a desolate land. After leaving his wife at the foot of Mount Pellegrino for dead, the king the husband suffers from the pangs of remorse for believing Wormwood to be guilty of adultery and rushes to find his wife and finds himself before the palace in the desolated land. He enters, sees a king seated in an armchair and takes a seat nearby. As for the doctor and his slave Ali, they go after the maid to slay her and they too end up in the palace in partial ruin and seat themselves across the two kings already seated.

The silence engulfing the room is pierced by the sound of a magic lantern which says "I want oil." A little oil cruet walks into the room, replenishes the oil reserve of the lantern and asks "Have you anything of interest to tell me?"

The lantern answers yes and begins to recount the long and interesting story of Wormwood. As the turns in the story touch the concerned person in the room, he hangs his head in shame and suffering while Ali shakes like a leaf. When the lantern reveals the truth behind the murder of Doctor's daughter, all three of them attack Ali and tear him to pieces and then they rush to the sofa where Wormwood still sleeps. "She's mine!" says the father king, "She's my daughter!" "She's mine!" counters the husband king, "She's my wife!" and the doctor adds in protest "She's mine! I saved her life!" (Calvino 567–568). Wormwood chooses to go with her husband and invites her father and the doctor to a celebration of her return and from then on they live as one, united, and happy family.

Giorgio Agamben quotes Pompeius Festus on a figure in Roman law which accorporates contrarieties and is therefore to open perplexing interpretations.

> The sacred man is the one whom the people have judged on account of a crime. It is not permitted to sacrifice this man, yet he who kills him will not be condemned for homicide; in the first tribunitian law, in fact, it is noted that "if someone kills the one who is sacred according to the plebiscite, it will not be considered homicide." This is why it is customary for a bad or impure man to be called sacred (Festus in Agamben *Homo Sacer* 71).

Simultaneously occupying the positions of the sacred and the profane, and outside both the heavenly and earthly laws, *homo sacer* (sacred man) has close ties to a political zone in which exception becomes the governing paradigm. Agamben calls this field of politics a kenomatic state where "an emptiness of law, and the idea of an originary indistinction" hold sway and thus constitute the nucleus of sovereign violence (Agamben *Homo Sacer* 77). The sovereign violence postulates "a zone of indistinction between law and nature, outside and inside, violence and law," and the sovereign is the one who renders the threshold between these binaries indistinguishable (Agamben 64). Between the figure of *homo sacer* and that of the sovereign there is a structural analogy: "the sovereign is the one with respect to whom all men are potentially *homines sacri*, and *homo sacer* is the one with respect to whom all men act as sovereigns." (Agamben 85). The outcasts, outlaws of a society, *homines sacri* could be regarded as the antitheses of law-abiding, law-protected citizens whose legal statuses are guaranteed by a sovereign (a monarch, a head of a state) power. The story of Remus and Romulus, the legendary twins of Rome, is a fine example that covers the both ends of the correlation between the *homo sacer* and the sovereign. In order to populate his burgeoning city, Romulus allotted a space, between the two forests, to refuges, "debitori insolventi, ladri, omicidi, fuggitivi di ogni sorta e specie" ("insolvent debtors, thieves, murders, fugitives of all sorts and species") (Ferro and

Monteleone 132), who sought protection from Rome. The *personae non gratae* of other cities were welcome prospects in Rome due to the insufficient sources of manpower and Romulus, in his capacity of the ultimate sovereign, allowed those abandoned by their native societies to be conferred Roman citizenships. The same Romulus, however, gave his consent to or personally carried out the execution of his twin brother Remus for breaching the sacred wall built around the city.

> Remo aveva superato il limite che avrebbe per sempre protetto lo spazio urbano, un limite posto sotto la tutela degli dèi. Quella violazione non era dunque solo una provocazione, ma un'empietà che andava espiata con la morte. Tale sarebbe stato da quel momento il castigo per chi avesse violato il confine sacro della città. (Ferro and Monteleone 128)
>
> Remus had transgressed the limit that would forever protect the urban space, a limit placed under the protection of the gods. That violation was therefore not just a provocation, but an impiety that had to be atoned for with death. Such would have been from that moment the punishment for those who violated the sacred boundary of the city.

In the tale "Wormwood" it is possible to identify narrative units and tropes that may dovetail with Giorgio Agamben's *homines sacri* and the legendary sovereign rulers of ancient Rome. Perhaps the best way to commence the analysis of the tale is by way of an interlude, however brief, on another Roman term *patria potestas* "power of a father" to better address the intertwining roles of daughter, wife, maid, father, husband, and master and to revert to the discussion on the matters of *homo sacer* and sovereignty. In the Roman family law, the power wielded by the male head of a family was vast indeed as the *patria* could exercise control not only over his children and grand-children but also over the distant relatives and even over the adopted members of his extended family. He was the supreme authority who could banish a member of his family and even had a right to inflict capital punishment. The rigidity of the practice was relaxed in the late Middle Ages as the sons' commercial activities gave them a degree of autonomy. Despite the mitigations, *patria potestas* "persisted unquestioned as the structural mainstay of family solidarity until the late seventeenth and eighteenth centuries" (Kirshner 89).

The familial relations in the tale, the filial relation between the king father and Wormwood, the conjugal relation between the king husband and Wormwood, the magisterial relation between the doctor and Wormwood, can be conjoined under the rubric of *pater familias*. The disagreement as to whom Wormwood belongs and as to her "rightful" social role, "daughter, wife, maid," might be traced to complexities that surround the issue of authority in a patriarchal family. The first king that is given as the father figure is the very embodiment of a *patria* who holds the absolute power of life and death, *merum imperium*, over a member of his dynasty. Wormwood's father, unfortunately, proves to be a despotic one who does not hesitate to have his child murdered for failing to meet his expectations and satisfy his desires and thus we have the first banishment of Wormwood to wilderness. The hermit who takes up the role of fatherhood and fulfills the missing benevolent part can be posited as counter to the first king, nevertheless, we can discern a fainter version of *imperium* since without consulting to Wormwood's opinion, he decides on the fate of her adopted daughter's life: "I am devoted to the child, so for her own good I'm happy for her to go to the palace. The education Your Majesty is able to offer her is a far cry from what a poor hermit could give her" (Calvino 564). The second king who becomes Wormwood's husband dotes upon her and displays signs of a perfect spouse except on the occasion when he bets on the chastity of his wife. Misled by the false statements of a knight, he attempts to kill her in a forlorn place. In the second king, we have the both ends of a father figure, benevolent and cruel, trustworthy and distrustful who once again exiles Wormwood to no-man's land. The doctor's role in the tale can be corresponded to that of the hermit on the grounds that he, just like the hermit, saves Wormwood's life and acts in the capacity of a foster father and Wormwood, in return for their goodwill, works as a maid and tends to their household chores.

In regards to the setting of the tale, it is possible to pursue a certain pattern of constant transition from urban areas to countryside and vice versa. This pattern traverses the storylines of the male characters given above and of Wormwood, the latter's movements, however, also entail the themes of death and life. Giorgio Agamben's *homo sacer* and sovereign power function on the assumption that the zones that respectively identify these two terms are characterized by indistinctions and thresholds. The "ban," "the original political relation" strips away the political rights and legal protections of a human being and thus reduces her/him to a bare life, to a "werewolf" status that is "neither man nor beast" (Agamben *Homo Sacer* 105). The sovereign, if he fancies, may use his unbridled power to set the boundaries between *polis* and wilderness and may banish a citizen to a wasteland of social death or confer life on a bare life and thus reinstate her/his social position. Officially, there are two sovereign figures in the tale, the father and the husband kings, yet their sovereignties are not absolute for there are two rulers in the first place and they have to return to the countryside to legitimize their holds on power. Truly, like the sovereigns of Agamben, they exercise their unassailable authority to expulsion and use their power to condemn Wormwood to *nuda vita* (bare life). Their visit to Wormwood in the dilapidated palace in the country, an imagery which might foreshadow the future ruin that awaits their kingdoms, can be read as an attempt to recover from a fatal mistake and to mend their broken family lines. It is not Wormwood, however, but the slave Ali who provides the opportunity for a family reunion and in this regard it may be argued that the position of *homo sacer* passes from Wormwood to the slave. Ali, similar to the fate of the nameless Moor in "The Moor's Bones" tale, is killed by being torn to pieces. Rene Girard believes that the victims that are subjected to an excessive violence serve a purpose in a society devoid of stable state institutions. They deflect and project the violence that "threatens to tear both the self and the community apart" and hence delays the danger of disintegration (Girard in Patterson 184). It can be argued that Ali's mutilated body performs such scapegoat function and diverts the direction of violence away from the inner circles of the sovereign family to a body whose death does not incur legal or political charges.

Like many tales with happy endings, the tale "Wormwood" concludes with a celebration of reconciliation and a wish to live as "one happily family" for a long time. Giorgio Agamben proposes that when the border separating biopolitics from thanatopolitics is effaced, when "the decision on life becomes a decision on death" and the sovereign moves into zones other than that of politics, the sovereign enters into "an ever more intimate symbiosis not only with the jurist but also with the doctor, the scientist, the expert, and the priest" (Agamben 122). The tale's final offers such vision of unification of institutions coalescing under the banner of one extended family thanks to the dismembered body of Ali who is killed with impunity.

Conclusion

The fall of Constantinople to Ottomans in 1453, the capital of the Eastern Roman Empire and a cardinal city of Christianity, sent shockwaves throughout Europe and the initial reactions of consternation, disbelief, and disappointment were mingled with the long simmering anxieties that Europe and Christianity would eventually succumb to Turks and Islam. The conquest rekindled the old fears the Islamic (Umayyad) Caliphate (661–750 C.E.) left when it held the Iberian Peninsula, Septimania (a region in southern France), the islands of Sicily and Malta under its control and set its eyes on conquering Rome and Vatican. The Caliphate's dreams of a decisive victory against its worldly and ecclesiastical arch-rival were eventually shattered, however, with the rapid rise of the Ottoman Empire and its advance into Europe during the fifteenth and sixteenth centuries the dormant apprehensions were revived and an old adversary was given a new name and a face. At this juncture, the sparse amount of writings on Turks, their origins, culture, and customs began to increase and the Renaissance scholars produced works whose tones wavered between praise and derision. Such ambiguous attitudes were bounded with and determined by the political agendas and milieus the works partook of and Turks were incorporated into the pre-existing postulations on Moorish and Muslim Others. Sometimes exalted and sometimes vituperated, the Ottomans, also representing Moors and Muslims, were called upon in times of dire need:

> ...Western culture, unable to solve the upheavals caused by the confrontation with the outside world (the Americas, the East) and by its (religious or political) divisions, described the Ottoman as a paradigmatic (infidel and cruel) enemy, but also as a positive example of unity, obedience and fidelity that the divided Western was not able to find. (Capriotti and Llopis 8–9)

The Italian epic poem *Orlando Furioso* by Ludovico Ariosto, a favorite work of Italo Calvino, was one of those scholarly works that was lenient with praise for the Ottomans while criticizing the decadence and disunity marring the Christian world. Despite its positive and egalitarian renditions of Saracens and Turks, the poem is "not detached from historical reality," and it participates in "the dominating discourse about the Turkish menace, reminding its readers about historical moments of conflict with the Muslims – with the Arabs in Jerusalem and in Sicily and with the Ottomans at the Balkans" (Lausten 121). It is also possible to identify a similar strand in Italian art, in iconographies decorating the walls and vaults of chapels and basilicas in Italy. In such visual representations, the

Turks and Saracens, usually depicted with darker skin tones, can be seen not as members of the congregation but as onlookers on the peripheries or as black figures of anti-Christ "frequently associated with devil and precociously identified with the Muslim religion" (Capriotti and Llopis 8–9).

It is possible to discern the extensive utilizations of mainstream and officially acknowledged representations of Turks and Moors in political, religious, administrative institutions and in cultural and literary productions. One could surmise that these representations would encapsulate and reflect the respective views of all strata in Italian society regardless of their class positions and affiliations. *Collisions, Deflections, and Conjunctions: The Representations of Turks and Moors in Italian Folktales* calls into question such generalizations and by way of offering a study of a literary field that has long been overlooked in European history and literature arrives at the following conclusions. Contrary to official perceptions that amalgamate Turks and Moors, the Italian folktales assign distinct roles and functions to these historical Others. The roles, unlike the ones promulgated by state to maintain order within its internal and external borders, are given in accordance with the interests and the aspirations of the Italian peasantry and at times are utilized against the deficiencies of state mechanism. The tales, somehow unexpectedly, also leave the parochial and national borders open for cultural and social crossings and provide a permeable, multilateral zone for encounters between the Occidental and the Oriental societies. Further studies would probably yield further or better results than the ones sketched by the present study, but I am of opinion that it will be a fine complementary work to the existing scholarship and a stepping stone for a multidisciplinary study with an extended scope. It would be interesting, for example, to conduct a research combining folk literature, Renaissance romances and accounts of *relazioni* (diplomatic dispatches) sent to and from the Republic of Venice. A study of such breadth and depth would definitely prove to be an arduous task to undertake, yet it may furnish us with parameters to study the notion of Otherness from multiple perspectives and enable us to see whether similar or different paradigms are employed in the descriptions and representations of Western (Italian, English, French, German, and Spanish) and Eastern (Jewish, Persian, Arabian, Greek, Slavic, and Turkish) identities.

Works Cited

Abulafia, David. "The South." *Italy in the Age of the Renaissance*, edited by John M. Najemy. Oxford University Press, 2004, pp. 208–226.

Agamben, Giorgio. *Homo Sacer: Sovereign Power and Bare Life*. Stanford University Press, 1998.

Agamben, Giorgio. *The Fire and the Tale*. Translated by Lorenzo Chiesa. Stanford University Press, Stanford, 2017.

Al-Rashīd, Ahmad. *Book of Gifts and Rarities*. Translated by Ghādah Ḥijjāwī Qaddūmī. Harvard University Press, 1996.

Althusser, Louis. *On the Reproduction of Capitalism: Ideology and Ideological State Apparatuses*. Translated by G. M. Goshgarian. Verso, 2014.

Arnold, David. "Gramsci and Peasant Subalternity in India." *Mapping Subaltern Studies and the Postcolonial*, edited by Vinayak Chaturvedi. Verso, 2000, pp. 24–49.

Auerbach, Erich. *Literary Language & Its Public in Late Latin Antiquity and in the Middle Ages*. Princeton University Press, 1993.

Bakhtin, Mikhail. *The Dialogic Imagination: The Four Essays*. The University of Texas Press, 1981.

Bakhtin, Mikhail. *Rabelais and His World*. Translated by Helene Iswolsky. Indiana University Press, 1984.

Barbero, Alessandro. "L'idea dello straniero in Italia: Italiani e stranieri," in *Straniero: L'invasore, l'esule, l' altro*. EncycloMedia Publishers, 2012.

Barthes, Roland. "An Introduction to the Structural Analysis of Narrative." *New Literary History*, vol. 6, no. 2, 1975, pp. 237–272.

Basile, Battista Giovanni. *Il Pentamerone Vol. I*. Translated by Richard Burton, Henry and Co. London, 1893.

Bassi, Shaul. *Shakespeare's Italy and Italy's Shakespeare: Place, "Race," Politics*. Palgrave Macmillan, 2016.

Baudrillard, Jean. *The System of Objects*. Verso, 2005.

Bauman, Richard. "Differential Identity and the Social Base of Folklore." *The Journal of American Folklore*, vol. 84, no. 331, 1971, pp. 31–41.

Ben-Amos, Dan. "Toward a Definition of Folklore in Context." *The Journal of American Folklore*, vol. 84, no. 331, 1971, pp. 3–15.

Berto, A. Luigi. *Christians and Muslims in Early Medieval Italy: Perceptions, Encounters, and Clashes*. Routledge, 2020.

Bettelheim, Bruno. *The Uses of Enchantment: The Meaning and Importance of Fairy Tales*. Vintage, 2010.

Bhabha, Homi. *The Location of Culture*. Routledge, 2004.

Boyer, M. Ruth. "Mythology, Folklore, and Psychoanalysis." *Psychology and Myth*, edited by Robert A. Segal. Garland Publishing, 1996, pp. 25–32.

Brackett, John. "Race and Rulership: Alessandro de' Medici, first Medici Duke of Florence, 1529–1537." *Black Africans in Renaissance Europe*, edited by T. F. Earle and K. J. P. Lowe. Cambridge University Press, 2005, pp. 303–325.

Braudel, Fernand. *The Mediterranean and the Mediterranean World in the Age of Philip II*. University of California Press, 1995.

Braudel, Fernand. *Out of Italy: Two Centuries of World Domination and Demise*. Europa Editions, 2019.

Brummett, Palmira. *Mapping the Ottomans: Sovereignty, Territory, and Identity in the Early Modern Mediterranean*. Cambridge University Press, 2015.

Bryce, Derek. "The Absence of Ottoman, Islamic Europe in Edward W. Said's Orientalism." *Theory, Culture & Society*, vol. 30, no. 1, 2013, pp. 99–121.

Calvino, Italo. *Italian Folktales*. Pantheon Books, 1980.

Capriotti, Giuseppe and Llopis, Borja. "Changing the Enemy, Visualizing the Other: The State of Art in Italian and Spanish Art Historiography." *Changing the Enemy, Visualizing the Other: Contacts between Muslims and Christians in the Early Modern Mediterranean Art*, edited by G. Capriotti and B. Llopis. Universita di Macerata, 2017, pp. 7–24.

Cereta, Laura. *The Collected Letters of a Renaissance Feminist*, edited and translated by Diana Robin. University of Chicago Press, 1997.

Chalupa, Cynthia. "Mirror." *The Greenwood Encyclopedia of Folktales and Fairy Tales, Vol. 1*, edited by Donald Haase. Greenwood Press, 2008, pp. 628–631.

Cinthio, Giraldi. "The Moor of Venice." *Hecatommithi III, 7*. Translated by J. E. Taylor. In Parentheses Publications, 2000.

Cipolla, Gaetano. *Siciliana: Studies on the Sicilian Ethos and Literature*. Legas, 2014.

Dalrymple, William. Foreword: The Porous Frontiers of Islam and Christendom: A Clash or Fusion of Civilisations? *Re-Orienting the Renaissance: Cultural Exchanges with the East*, edited by Gerald MacLean. Palgrave Macmillan, 2005, pp. ix–xxiii.

Darovec, Darko. *A Brief History of Istra*. ALA Publications, 1998.

Davis, C. Robert. *Christian Slaves, Muslim Masters: White Slavery in the Mediterranean, the Barbary Coast, and Italy, 1500–1800*. Palgrave Macmillan, 2004.

De Certeau, Michel. *The Writing of History*. Translated by Tom Conley. Columbia University Press, 1988.

Deleuze, Gilles. *Desert Islands and Other Texts, 1953–1974*. Translated by Michael Taormina. Semiotext(e), 2004.

Derrida, Jacques. *Of Grammatology*. The Johns Hopkins University Press, 1997.

Derrida, Jacques. "Differance." *Literary Theory: An Anthology*, edited by Julie Rivkin and Michael Ryan. Blackwell Publishing, 2004, pp. 278–299.

Derrida, Jacques. *Specters of Marx: The State of the Debt, the Work of Mourning and the New International*. Routledge, 2006.

De Vivo, Filippo. "How to Read Venetian *Relazioni*." *Renaissance and Reformation/Renaissance et Réforme*, vol. 34, no. 1–2, 2011, pp. 25–59.

Dogra, Sapna. "The Thirty-One Functions in Vladimir Propp's Morphology of the Folktale: An Outline and Recent Trends in the Applicability of the Proppian Taxonomic Model." *Rupkatha Journal on Interdisciplinary Studies in Humanities*, vol. IX, no. 2, 2017, pp. 410–419.

Dorson, M. Richard. "Current Folklore Theories." *Current Anthropology*, vol. 4, no. 1, 1963, pp. 93–112.

Dorson, M. Richard. "Introduction: Concepts of Folklore and Folklife Studies." *Folklore and Folklife: An Introduction*, edited by Richard M. Dorson, The University of Chicago Press, 1972, pp. 1–50.

Dundes, Alan. "The Devolutionary Premise in Folklore Theory." *Journal of the Folklore Institute*, vol. 6, no. 1, 1969, pp. 5–19.

Dundes, Alan. *Interpreting Folklore*. Indiana University Press, 1980.

Dundes, Alan. *Parsing through Customs: Essays by a Freudian Folklorist*. The University of Wisconsin Press, 1987.

Dundes, Alan. "The Motif-Index and the Tale Type Index: A Critique." *Journal of Folklore Research*, vol. 34, no. 3, 1997, pp. 195–202.

Eco, Umberto. *On Ugliness*. Random House Incorporated, 2011.

Eldem, Edhem. *Consuming the Orient*. Ottoman Bank Archives and Research Centre, 2007.

Epstein, A. Steven. *Speaking of Slavery: Color, Ethnicity, and Human Bondage in Italy*. Cornell University Press, 2001.

Ferro, Licia and Monteleone, Maria. *Miti Romani: Il racconto*. Einaudi, 2014.

Firges, Pascal and Graf, Tobias. Introduction. *Well-Connected Domains: Towards an Entangled Ottoman History*, edited by P. Firges et. al., Brill, 2014, pp. 1–11.

Fischer, J. L. "The Sociopsychological Analysis of Folktales." *Current Anthropology*, vol. 4, no. 3, 1963, pp. 235–295.

Fontana, Benedetto. *Hegemony and Power: On the Relation Between Gramsci and Machiavelli.* University of Minnesota Press, 1993.

Formica, Marina. *Lo specchio turco: Immagini dell'altro e riflessi del sé nella cultura italiana d'età moderna.* Donzelli, 2012.

Gabrieli, Francesco and Scerrato, Umberto. *Gli Arabi in Italia Cultura, contatti e tradizioni.* Garzanti-Scheiwiller, 1985.

Gencarella, O., Stephen. "Gramsci, Good Sense, and Critical Folklore Studies." *Journal of Folklore Research*, vol. 47, no. 3, 2010, pp. 221–252.

Graf, Tobias. *The Sultan's Renegades: Christian-European Converts to Islam and the Making of the Ottoman Elite, 1575–1610.* Oxford University Press, 2017.

Gramsci, Antonio. *Selections from Cultural Writings*, edited by David Forgacs. Lawrence & Wishar, 1985.

Gramsci, Antonio. *The Antonio Gramsci Reader: Selected Writings 1916–1935*, edited by David Forgacs. NYU Press, 2000.

Greenblatt, Stephen. "Towards a Poetics of Culture." *The New Historicism*, edited by Harold Veeser. Routledge, 1989, pp. 1–14.

Grosz, Elizabeth. *Volatile Bodies: Toward a Corporeal Feminism.* Indiana University Press, 1994.

Guicciardini, Francesco and Machiavelli, Niccolo. *The Sweetness of Power: Machiavelli's Discourses and Guicciardini's Considerations*, edited by James Atkinson. Northern Illinois University Press, 2002.

Harle, Peter. "Structuralism." *Folklore Forum*, vol. 30, no. 1–2, 1999, pp. 9–19.

Holland, P. Sharon. *Raising the Dead: Readings of Death and (Black) Subjectivity.* Duke University Press, 2000.

İnalcık, Halil. *Rönesans Avrupası: Türkiye'nin Batı Medeniyetiyle Özdeşleşme Süreci.* Türkiye İş Bankası Yayınları, 2013.

Jameson, Fredric. "The Vanishing Mediator: Narrative Structure in Max Weber," *New German Critique*, vol. 1, 1973, pp. 52–82.

Jansen, William. "The Esoteric-Exoteric Factor in Folklore." *Fabula*, vol. 2, no. 2, 1959, pp. 205–211.

Jones, Ernest. *Essays in Applied Psychoanalysis.* The Hogarth Press, 1951.

Kaplan, H. D. Paul. "Black Turks: Venetian Artists and Perceptions of Ottoman Ethnicity." *The Turk and Islam in the Western Eye, 1450 – 1750*, edited by James G. Harper. Routledge, 2016, pp. 41–66.

Kast, Verena. *Folktales as Therapy.* Fromm International, 1995.

Kirshner, Julius. "Family and Marriage: A Socio-legal Perspective." *Italy in the Age of the Renaissance: 1300–1550*, edited by John M. Najemy. Oxford University Press, 2004, pp. 82–102.

Kopf, David. "Hermeneutics versus History." *The Journal of Asian Studies*, vol. 39, no. 3, 1980, pp. 495–506.

Kreutz, Barbara. *Before the Normans: Southern Italy in the Ninth and Tenth Centuries*. University of Pennsylvania Press, 1991.

Lausten, Pia. "Saracens and Turks in Ariosto's Orlando Furioso: Sheer Imagination or Allusions to Reality?" *Nordic Journal of Renaissance Studies*, vol. 16, 2019, pp. 97–126.

Lévi-Strauss, Claude. "The Structural Study of Myth." *The Journal of American Folklore*, vol. 68, no. 270, 1955, pp. 428–444.

Lévi-Strauss, Claude. *Structural Anthropology*. University of Chicago Press, 1983.

Lewis, Bernard. *Islam and the West*. Oxford University Press, 1993.

Lombardi-Satriani, Luigi. "Folklore as Culture of Contestation." *Journal of the Folklore Institute*, vol. 11, no. 1–2, 1974, pp. 99–121.

Lowe, Kate. "The Stereotyping of black Africans in Renaissance Europe." *Black Africans in Renaissance Europe*, edited by T. F. Earle and K. J. P. Lowe. Cambridge University Press, 2005, pp. 17–47.

Lucy, Niall. *A Derrida Dictionary*. Blackwell Publishing, 2004.

Macherey, Pierre. *A Theory of Literary Production*. Routledge, 1978.

MacKenzie, John. *Orientalism: History, Theory and the Arts*. Manchester University Press, 1995.

MacLean, Gerald. "Introduction." *Re-Orienting the Renaissance: Cultural Exchanges with the East*, edited by Gerald MacLean. Palgrave Macmillan, 2005, pp. 1–28.

Makdisi, Ussama. "Ottoman Orientalism." *The American Historical Review*, vol. 107, no. 3, 2002, pp. 768–796.

Marx, Karl. *The Eighteenth Brumaire of Louis Bonaparte*. Mondial, 2005.

Matar, Nabil. *Turks, Moors, and Englishmen in the Age of Discovery*. Columbia University Press, 1999.

McKee, Sally. "Domestic Slavery in Renaissance Italy." *Slavery and Abolition*, vol. 29, no. 3, 2008, pp. 305–326.

Meletinsky, Eleazar. "Structural-Typological Study of Folktales." *Soviet Structural Folkloristics, vol. 1*, edited by Pierre Maranda. Mouton, 1974, pp. 19–53.

Mitler, Louis. "The Genoese in Galata: 1453–1682." *International Journal of Middle East Studies*, vol. 10, no. 1, 1979, pp. 71–91.

Neumann, Iver and Welsh, Jennifer. "The Other in European Self-definition: An Addendum to the Literature on International Society." *Review of International Studies*, vol. 17, no. 04, 1991, pp. 327–348.

Niccoli, Ottavia. *Prophecy and People in Renaissance Italy*. Translated by Lydia G. Cochrane. Princeton University Press, 1990.

Noyes, Dorothy. "The Social Base of Folklore." *A Companion to Folkore*, edited by Regina F. Bendix and Galit Hasan-Rokem. Wiley-Blackwell, 2012, pp. 13–39.

Origo, Iris. "The Domestic Enemy: The Eastern Slaves in Tuscany in the Fourteenth and Fifteenth Centuries." *Speculum*, vol. 30, no. 3, 1955, pp. 321–366.

Pamuk, Orhan. *The White Castle*. Translated by Victoria Holbrook. Vintage Books, 1998.

Patterson, Orlando. *Rituals of Blood: The Consequences of Slavery in Two American Centuries*. Basic Books, 1999.

Petrarca, Francesco. *Opere di Francesco Petrarca*, edited by Emilio Bigi. Mursia, 1966.

Pizzi, Katia. *A City in Search of an Author: The Literary Identity of Trieste*. Continuum, 2001.

Propp, Vladimir. *Morphology of the Folktale*. The American Folklore Society and Indiana University, 1968.

Propp, Vladimir. *Theory and History of Folktale*. University of Minnesota Press, 1997.

Purkiss, Diane. *The Witch in History: Early Modern and Twentieth Century Representations*. Routledge, 1996.

Rickards, Labarga, Scano, et al. "Genetic History of the Population of Sicily." *Human Biology*, vol. 70, no. 4, 1998, pp. 699–714.

Rosenberg, A. Bruce. *Folklore and Literature: Rival Siblings*. The University of Tennessee Press, 1991.

Rossi, Nassim. *Italian Renaissance Depictions of the Ottoman Sultan: Nuances in the Function of Early Modern Italian Portraiture*. Columbia University, PhD dissertation, 2013.

Royle, Nicholas. *Jacques Derrida*. Routledge, 2003.

Röhrich, Lutz. "Introduction." *Fairy Tales and Society: Illusion, Allusion, and Paradigm*, edited by Ruth B. Bottigheimer. University of Pennsylvania Press, 1989, pp. 1–12.

Röhrich, Lutz. *Folktales and Reality*. Translated by Peter Tokofsky. Indiana UP, 1991.

Rumpf, Marianne, et. al. "The Legends of Bertha in Switzerland." *Journal of the Folklore Institute*, vol. 14, no. 3, 1977, pp. 181–195.

Said, Edward. *Orientalism: Western Conceptions of the Orient*. Penguin Books, 1994.

Said, Edward. "Introduction." *Mimesis: The Representation of Reality in Western Literature*. Princeton University Press, 2003, pp. i–xxiv.

Satriani, Lombardi Luigi. *La stanza degli specchi*. Meltemi Editore, 2005.

Tateo, Francesco. "L'ideologia umanistica e il simbolo 'immane' di Otranto." *Otranto 1480: atti del convegno internazionale di studio promosso in occasione del V centenario della caduta di Otranto ad opera dei Turchi, vol. 1*, edited by Cosimo Damiano Fonseca. Galatina Congedo Editore, 1986, pp. 153–180.

Thompson, Stith. *The Folktale*. The University of California Press, 1977.

Uysal, E. Ahmet. "Street Cries in Turkey." *Journal of American Folklore*, vol. 81, no. 321, 1968, pp. 193–215.

Vaughan, M. Virginia. *Othello: A Contextual History*. Cambridge University Press, 1994.

Von Sydow, Carl Wilhelm. *Selected Papers on Folklore*. Ayer Company Publishers, 1977.

Wortham, M. Simon. "Supplement." The Derrida Dictionary. Continuum, 2010, pp. 203–304.

Zipes, Jack. *Fairy Tales and the Art of Subversion*. Routledge, 1991.

Zipes, Jack. *Breaking the Magic Spell: Radical Theories of Folk and Fairy Tales*. The University Press of Kentucky, 2002.

Žižek, Slavoj. *Žižek's Jokes*. The MIT Press, 2018.